Cover design by Thomas F. Maxson
Cover layout and production by Ryan T. Maxson

The cover design includes a photo of the Michael Keropian model sculpture of Chief Nimham, with both photo and model sculpture courtesy of Mr. Keropian. For more information on the sculpture, how to contribute to the full-scale casting of this amazing work of art, and to learn of Mr. Keropian's many other projects and works, please visit his website at: http://www.keropiansculpture.com

The cover design also includes photos of Mount Nimham Civil War veterans William Niles Dean, his brother John Haviland Dean, and William D. Light. These photos are provided courtesy of the Kent Historical Society, and we would also like to thank the late Mrs. Addison Hopkins, the niece of the Dean brothers. For more information regarding the Kent Historical Society and their programs and activities, please visit their web page at: http://www.townofkentny.gov/historian.htm

In May of 2009, the Daniel Nimham Statue Committee was formed as an "ad hoc" committee of the Kent Historical Society. The purpose of this ad hoc committee is to plan and oversee the solicitation of financial and public support leading to the creation of Mr. Keropian's sculpture for both the Wappinger Memorial and the entrance to the Kent Town Hall Complex. For more information, or to contribute to this worthy endeavor, please contact the author at: thomasmaxson@highlandspreservation.org

The Kent Conservation Advisory Committee completed the restoration of the fire tower atop the mountain in 2005. This volunteer organization advises the Town Board on conservation and open space utilization issues, helping to preserve Kent's natural, rural character. For more information regarding their activities, including their annual hiking series, please visit their website at: http://www.townofkentny.gov/conservation.htm

The *Nimham Mountain Singers* is an organization dedicated to preserving Native American Indian culture, traditions, and spirituality. This organization performs at the annual Daniel Nimham Pow Wow held at the Putnam County Veteran's Park, located in the shadow of the mountain, an extraordinary event which they also organize each year. They also perform at schools, civic events and other pow wows, and offer a complete educational program of drumming, traditional songs and dances, and Wappinger cultural history designed for children and adults. For more information, or to contribute to the creation of the Chief Daniel Nimham statue, please visit their website at: http://www.nimham .com/

MOUNT NIMHAM:
THE RIDGE OF PATRIOTS
HISTORICAL TIMELINE

Including Coles Mills and Big Hill

The first in a series of historical timelines covering the people, places and events in the town of Kent, Putnam County, New York

By Thomas F. Maxson
Chairman
Highlands Preservation, Inc.
A Non-Profit Organization Dedicated to Preserving Historic and Prehistoric Sites in the Hudson Highlands

Rangerville Press
Kent, New York
A Division of Robert Sterling Publishing, Inc.
Molokai, Hawaii

MOUNT NIMHAM:
THE RIDGE OF PATRIOTS
HISTORICAL TIMELINE

Printed in the United States of America

First Printing: July 2009

ISBN 978-0-578-02581-0

For my loving and patient wife Robin, our wonderful children Andrea and Ryan, Jason, and Ranger.

Mount Nimham: The Ridge of Patriots
Historical Timeline

Acknowledgements

The author wishes to acknowledge the assistance of the following individuals and organizations in the compilation of this history of Mt. Nimham, Coles Mills and Big Hill: Gil *'Cryinghawk'* and Penny *'Painted Pony'* Tarbox, Joan Rickert and Evan Shatz, Ed and Trish Illiano, Jim and Wilma Baker, George and Kaye Baum, Robin L. Maxson, Ryan T. Maxson, Lou Tartaro, the Putnam County Historian's Office (County Historian Patricia Houser, former County Historian Allan Warnecke, Deputy Historian Sallie Sypher, Carol Bailey, Christina Mucciolo, Cathy Wargas, and Reggie White), Bettymarie Light Behr, Tom Breslin, Brian Flood, the Kent Historical Society, the Kent Public Library, the Patterson Library, the Reed Memorial Library, Michael Keropian, Kathy Kane, Richard Othmer, Jr., the late Rev. Floyd B. Fisher, the late Richard Muscarella, the late Stephen Kenneth Townsend and his wife, the late Ella Hyatt Pombo Townsend, Adelbert "Snookie" Adams, Ralph Merritt, Lynn E. Greenwood, Sr., PlanPutnam, Vincent Dacquino, Evan Pritchard, the late Mrs. Addison Hopkins, the late Karen Tuchman, and George C. Whipple, III.

The author also wishes to acknowledge the following individuals and organizations who have helped to protect and preserve our sacred mountain: Gil *'Cryinghawk'* and Penny *'Painted Pony'* Tarbox, Brooke *'Wolf That Runs With Pony'* Taylor, Wendy *'Walks Soft'* Mathewson, Joan Rickert and Evan Shatz, Ed and Trish Illiano, Jim and Wilma Baker, George and Kaye Baum, Kathy Doherty, Lou Tartaro, Richard Othmer, Jr., Mike Tierney, Annmarie Baisley, Ray Maneiro, Jeff Green, Arne Nordstrom, the Kent Town Board (past and present), the Kent Conservation Advisory Committee, Michael Keropian, Marty Collins, Beth Herr, Sue Kotzur, Mike Troy, Vincent Dacquino, Evan Pritchard, Robin L. Maxson, Ryan T. Maxson, Andrea E. Maxson, the Croton Watershed Clean Water Coalition, Riverkeeper, Dr. Parker Gambino, New York State Senator Vincent Leibell, New York State Assemblywoman Sandy Galef, James Tierney, Ann Fanizzi, Lynn E. Greenwood, Sr., the Kent Rod and Gun Club, James Shearwood, The Gipsy Trail Club, the Clearpool Education Center, the Putnam County Land Trust, the New England Antiquities Research Association (NEARA), PLAN-Kent, The Friends of Mt. Nimham, Preserve Putnam, the Kent Police Department, the NYS Forest Rangers, the New York State Historic Preservation Office, and especially Chief Daniel Nimham, Captain Abraham Nimham, and all the other patriots, and their families, who sacrificed so much for our continued independence.

Mount Nimham: The Ridge of Patriots
Historical Timeline

Table of Contents

Mount Nimham: The Ridge of Patriots
Historical Timeline

Introduction

Mount Nimham is a sprawling promenade located in the middle of the town of Kent, and represents the southwestern wall of the valley known as Whang Hollow. It is the highest point in the town of Kent, a locale well known for its steep slopes and high ridge lines. Mt. Nimham boasts extremely steep slopes, rocky outcrops, deep gorges and high ridges, glacial erratics and boulder fields, and it provides magnificent vistas of the surrounding countryside. To the east is found Whang Hollow, including Pine Pond, Townsend Ridge, Barrett Hill, Beaver Hill, and Hemlock Ledge; to the north, Stockholm Hill and the Little and Big Buck Mountains; to the west, Clear Pool and the Boyd Reservoir and Dam; and to the south, Coles Mills and the West Branch Reservoir. The mountain itself contains many extended arms and legs, with multiple levels and ridge lines, spreading out in all directions.

Accessible by Gipsy Trail Road, Mt. Nimham Court, Beach Road (Maynard Road), Coles Mills Road and Old Cole Shears Road, this treasured resource was home to the Nochpeem tribe, and its predecessors, for thousands of years prior to the arrival of the European explorers, fur traders, and settlers. The Nochpeem were part of the Wappinger Confederacy, which covered the eastern side of the Hudson River within the lower Hudson River Valley. The mountain is named after the greatest Wappinger Sachem and true American hero, the patriot Chief Daniel Nimham, who fought, and gave his life, for American independence, despite having lost his ancestral homeland to the Philipse family and the very settlers he was fighting for. It is reported that Chief Nimham came to this mountain on every birthday he celebrated, climbing to the top to proclaim all that could be seen as the ancestral homeland of the Wappinger. He always sought peaceful means of settling his disagreements with the elitist landowners, appealing to the Colonial and English Courts, who failed to acknowledge the Natives' land-owning rights, instead recognizing fraudulent deeds presented by the Philipse family. Following Nimham's death in pursuit of our independence on August 31, 1778 at the Battle of Kingsbridge, the remaining Wappinger were gradually forced out of this area forever. They eventually assimilated into other tribes.

The other patriots who share in the history of Mount Nimham, starting at the southernmost end of the mountain, include: Captain Solomon Hopkins and his son, Jeremiah; Captain Elisha Cole Jr. and his sons, Elisha III, Ebenezer, Joseph and Daniel, and the son of Elisha III, Reuben; heading northward up Coles Mills Road, Jacob VanScoy, Lt. Thomas Russell and his brothers, John, James, and Robert; heading still further north, James Smalley and his sons James Jr., Isaiah and Zachariah; then Lt. Col. Elijah Townsend and his brother, General James Townsend; and finally at the northernmost end of the mountain, Samuel Hawkins.

Following the American victory at Saratoga in 1777, and the passage of the Act of Attainder by the New York Colonial Legislature, Lot No. 5 of the Upper Highlands Patent of the Philipse Patent, including the Mt. Nimham area, was seized from the Mary Philipse Morris family, and sold off to the tenant farmers living on the mountain. Over the ensuing 150 years, the mountain and surrounding area was dominated by the farms of the Smalley, Townsend, Russell, Brown, Wixon, Hawkins, Light, Hopkins, Ferris, Cole, Tompkins, and Dean families. During this time, it became known as "Smalley Hill," in recognition of the majority ownership of the mountain, and in remembrance of the four members of the Smalley family who served as patriots during the Revolution.

The original old growth forest was cleared to create planting and grazing fields, with the wood used to build shelters, fuel fireplaces, and provide a source of revenue for the farmers. In addition, mining operations were conducted to remove serpentine and mineral deposits, particularly arsenic. The mountain was eventually renamed for the great Wappinger Sachem, Chief Daniel Nimham, in recognition of his supreme sacrifice for our independence. When farming declined in the early 1900s, New York State purchased the old farmland and eventually designated the majority of the mountain as a multiple use recreation area. A road to the top of the mountain was built by the CCC in 1940. That same year, the CCC built the steel fire tower at the top, which was recently restored by the Kent Conservation Advisory Committee. The mountain has returned to a "new growth" forest, enjoyed by both local residents and visitors from far and wide.

This author has chosen to tell the story of Mount Nimham using an historical timeline approach. By employing this style, the context in which these events occurred becomes more evident as opposed to a purely narrative approach. This is especially important in terms of understanding the demise of the local Native American Indian population, which occurred due to the numerous wars, epidemics, and fraudulent land grabs which systematically weakened their population numbers and their ability to withstand the onslaught of the new European entrants settling upon their ancestral homeland.

The author has done his best to rely upon purely factual sources to recount the history of the mountain, and those who called it their home. Any errors or omissions in the retelling of this history, though unintentional, are apologized for in advance.

Finally, the author wishes to echo the expressed desire of the historian William S. Pelletreau, when he wrote:

"With these words, the author lays down his pen, and concludes the task which has so long been a pleasure. He ventures to hope that his labor will be appreciated long after he is dust, and that whoever attempts a similar task, in the future, will accept his base although they may enlarge his building."

Chapter 1

Mount Nimham in the Prehistoric Era

Born from the uplift created by a series of orogenies, and shaped by extended periods of glacial activity, Mount Nimham became the highest point in what would eventually be known as the town of Kent. Following the last glacial period, which finally ended approximately 12,500 years ago, plant life returned, followed by animal life, and finally human life migrated into this area. The Native people would live in this, their ancestral homeland, in relative peace and prosperity for thousands of years . . .

Most scientists agree that the earth was formed approximately 4.6 billion years ago, from elements ejected as a result of the "big bang" and the birth of the universe. At first, there were no oceans and no oxygen in the atmosphere. The earth was bombarded by planetoids and other material left over from the initial formation of our solar system. This external bombardment, combined with extreme heat from radioactive breakdown, residual heat, and heat from the pressure of contraction, caused the planet at this early stage to be fully molten. But eventually temperatures plummeted, and the crust of the planet was accumulated on a solid surface. Subsequent large impacts created localized melting, and a series of molten and cooling periods continued. Gases formed by the emission of steam and other volcanic releases completed what was known as the second atmosphere. Water was imported from additional asteroid collisions. Eventually, the planet cooled, and the resulting rainfall helped to create the oceans, approximately 4.2 billion years ago.

Geologists agree that the oldest rocks on earth formed approximately 3.9 billion years ago. And the dynamics of our changing planet was further enhanced by the forces of plate tectonics, with new mountains forming, old mountains being worn down, and volcanic activity melting and reshaping the original rock formations.

A series of orogenies (Greek for "mountain building") occurred in which these continental plates and other land masses collided with each other, forcing the land to fold upward and creating the original mountain ranges and highlands in this area. The early stages of alteration occurred in a mountain-building episode that affected the entire eastern margin of North America. This mountain-building episode is collectively known as the Grenville Orogeny, which ended roughly a billion years ago. During this period older rocks and sediments were subjected to deep burial and metamorphic alteration.

A long period of uplift and erosion followed the Grenville Orogeny, yet later periods of mountain-building related to the formation of the Appalachian Mountains also contributed to the alteration and tectonic deformation of these rocks. Two smaller mountain-building episodes occurred in early Paleozoic time: The Taconic Orogeny and the Acadian Orogeny. The Taconic Orogeny began in Cambrian time (about 480 million years ago) and ended around Late Ordovician time (approximately 440 million years ago). During the Taconic Orogeny a small landmass, similar in size to modern Japan, was absorbed onto the North American continent in the southern New England area. Before and during this orogeny, sedimentary deposits formed on the margins of both the North American continent, and within an intervening deep marine basin. Today, these sedimentary rocks form the core of the Taconic Mountains and highlands east of the Hudson River, generally north of the Tappan Zee Bridge.

Large, significant glaciations occurred during the late Proterozoic eon (800-600 million years ago), the Pennsylvanian and Permian epochs (350-250 million years ago), and the late Neogene to Quaternary periods (the last 4 million years).

The glacial epoch or Pleistocene Ice Age (1.65M-12,000 years ago) created the uniquely beautiful Hudson Valley region and carved out its prominent curving ridges, sculpted hills and lake basins. The ice sheet that once covered this region in innumerable small glaciers moved slowly over a nearly one-million year period through the highland areas, forming and reforming, while deepening valleys, steepening hillsides, flattening mountain tops and excavating natural basins for the numerous lakes and gorges that imprint this area. Flowing silently and slowly further down the valleys, rock fragments from this long excavation deposited ridges of stones and boulders along valley margins. The glacier would form, advance, recede, and then re-form again. Since this area was near the end of the last glacial advance, the receding glacier deposited the innumerable "glacial erratics" and boulder fields so commonly found here.

The PaleoIndian period (12,000 - 8,000 B.C.) is the time humans first came to the southeastern New York region. The original migration theory assumed that these early inhabitants crossed the land bridge connecting East Asia to the western side of the North American continent. This theory states that these cave-dwelling "ancient Indians" came to the Hudson Valley approximately 12,000 years ago, after the Wisconsin Glacier had receded.

5

This is a time 5,500 years before the building of the pyramids in Egypt, 4,500 years before the invention of the wheel, 3,000 years before the development of river valley civilizations, 1,000 years before the prevalent use of pottery, and long before the use of agriculture in other parts of the world.

But it must be pointed out that there is a great deal of dispute regarding the Siberian land bridge migration theory. For one thing, some Native American Indians find this migration theory a bit offensive, as they believe their ancestors were always here in their ancestral homeland. In fact, Lenni-Lenape legends passed down through the generations indicate that their ancestors were here in their ancestral homelands after the first iteration of the Wisconsin Glacier arrived in this area. This legend indicates that the "first people" moved out of the area when the glacier advanced again, then returned once the ice sheet had finally receded (Tarbox).

And yet another theory points to the cave-dwelling PaleoIndians in the Eastern U.S. as having originated from Spain, France, Eastern Europe, and Russia. This theory is based on the difference in "Clovis Points" (sharpened tools originally discovered in Clovis, N.M.) between eastern North American Native American Indians versus their western counterparts. The eastern Clovis Points are much more similar to the Southern European version rather than to the western Native version. The western Native American Clovis Points more closely resemble those found in East Asia. This theory has the eastern cave dwellers crossing the glacial ice sheet over the Northern Atlantic from Britain to Greenland, and over to the North American continent (Tarbox; USDA Forest Service).

The Archaic period (8,000 - 1,700 BC) refers to a time prior to the intro-duction of horticulture and pottery manufacture, and is divided into Early, Middle, and Late periods. During the Archaic period, the environment changed from a pine dominated forest to an increasingly deciduous one which achieved a modern character by 2,000 BC (Boesch). The Transitional period (1,700 - 1,000 BC) saw a gradual change in Archaic lifestyles with the development of "Woodland" period traits. The Woodland period (1,000 BC - AD 1,600), which is characterized by the use of pottery and a reliance on horticulture, is divided into Early, Middle, and Late periods (Funk; Boesch).

The Hudson Valley Native American Indian tribes were part of the Algonquin Confederacy, also known as "Algunkeean" (Pritchard), and were part of the Lenni-Lenape culture consisting of the Munsee (on the western side of the Hudson), Mahican (from Rhinebeck north to Albany), and the Wappinger Confederacies (from Manhattan north to Poughkeepsie, on the eastern side of the Hudson River). This area, which includes Westchester, Putnam, and Dutchess Counties, was the home of the Wappinger Confederacy (meaning "easterner" or "east of the river"). The tribe which was specifically located in what is now Putnam County was the "Nochpeem," who were bordered by the "Kitchawank" to the south and the "Wiccopee," (meaning "Nut tree, or shady place"), a sub-tribe of the Nochpeem, to the north (Tarbox, 4). In fact, the Croton River was known as the "Kill of Kitchawang" in the late 1600s and 1700s. The Wappinger homeland extended from the Hudson River (which is actually a tidal estuary, and was originally known by the Native American Indians as the Mahikanittuk or the Shatauc River, or the "river that flows both ways") east to the Housatonic River.

The Wappinger Confederacy included the following sub-nations or tribes:

- *Appawamis*, from the Mamaroneck area;
- *Candatowa*, located in the extreme western portion of Fairfield County, Connecticut, into the eastern halves of Dutchess and Putnam Counties;
- *Cantitoe*, from the Bedford area;
- *Kitchawank* (alternately spelled Kitchawang, or Kitchawong), who made their home in northern Westchester County;
- *Mattawan*, from the Fishkill area;
- *Nochpeem*, located primarily in the Kent and Carmel area;
- *Sint Sink* (alternately spelled Sinsink), located on the eastern side of the Hudson River between Tarrytown and Croton;
- *Siwanoy* (or Sinanoy), located in the area from Hellgate east to Norwalk, Connecticut;
- *Taquam*, from the Patterson-Pawling area;
- *Wappinger* (or Waping), located on the east side of the Hudson River between Wappinger Falls and Poughkeepsie;
- *Wechquaesgeek* (or Wiechquaeskeck, Wickquaskeek), located on the east side of the Hudson River between the Bronx and Tarrytown (Tarbox).

The Wappinger people spoke a unique proto-Algonquin dialect of the Renneiu language, with a hard "R" dialect (Tarbox, 1; Sultzman). Many of the early settlers in Kent either previously lived in or passed through Westchester on their way northward. These settlers were familiar with the Kitchawang tribe from northern Westchester, and mistakenly thought the Native Americans in what is now the town of Kent were of that tribe. Although the Kitchawang were part of the Wappinger Confederacy, we now know that the local Native Americans in the Kent area were of the Nochpeem (Tarbox, 1; Ruttenber). One account has the word Nochpeem as meaning "a misty place" (Pritchard). Another account defines it as corresponding to "keeper of the secret" (Fisher).

The Wappinger manufactured a superior form of wampum, including copper elements, which they traded with the other tribes. There appears to have been limited conflict between tribes before European contact, even as tribes vied for this valuable commodity. However, there were periodic raids by European slavers during the 1500s. As a result, the Wappinger were forced to make more extensive military preparations than the norm. Besides their villages, most of the Wappinger had at least two "castles," or forts, where they could retreat when threatened. They usually resided in these forts during the winter months.

Native American Indian villages were usually positioned on the side of a hill, facing south or east, and within easy access to water (Fisher). The village would usually be found on a ridge above the wetland, stream or lake. The Nochpeem's main villages were known as Canopus (Canpopus), Keskistkonk, Nochpeem, and Pasquasheck (Sultzman). As a rule, the Wappinger only lived in their villages during the warmer months and moved to their forts for the winter. Within the Mt. Nimham area, it is believed there were settlements on the eastern base of Mt. Nimham, south of Pine Pond (Tarbox, 1), on the western side of the mountain on Coles Shears Road, and in the area west of Boyd's Dam now covered by the reservoir (Blake, 327), although recent information points to a site along Tompkins Road (see Illustration 1). Each settlement had single-family lodges, some as long as 50 feet in length. As late as the 1930s, there were still Nochpeem lodges or forts found on the top of Mt. Nimham and on its western face. Even at that late date, a few still had their roofs in place, while the others were in a state of disrepair (Townsend).

Of the Wappinger Confederacy tribes, the Nochpeem were considered to be especially fierce warriors and very tough opponents in any conflict. They were the ones entrusted with holding any captives during conflicts with other tribes, and later during the wars with the European transplants as well.

According to Sultzman, the Wappinger were organized into sachem-ships where, in most cases, the authority of the sachem and council (composed of clan chiefs) extended over only a few villages and was limited mostly to resolving problems and disputes. Councils of the individual sachems were only held as required to deal with common problems. However, in times of war, leadership was given to a war chief, whose authority was absolute for the duration of the conflict. A greater degree of organization was not required, since the Wappinger generally lived in peace with most of their neighbors. The culture of these early inhabitants seemed to be based on a greater degree of cooperation and respect toward their peers, as opposed to the Europeans who were in constant competition with each other.

These Native American Indians believed that the land belonged to the Great Spirit, the Creator, "Manitou" (based on an ancient word meaning "spirit"), who allowed them to use it (Pritchard). Manitou was considered the Supreme Being, and lived in everything. The water, trees, animals, rocks, and the moon and the stars were all attributed to, and attributes of, the Great Spirit. They would pay homage to the Great Spirit and recite visions during the "Big House" ceremony. This sacred ceremony was thought to benefit all people, to avert natural catastrophe, and to hold the members of the tribe together (Tarbox). The unique glacial erratic formation known as "Hawk Rock," located east of Pine Pond and just west of Horsepound Brook, was most likely viewed by the Nochpeem as a physical manifestation of the Great Spirit, and would have been a very important spiritual center for them (the hawk was a symbol of wisdom, strength and courage). This spiritual treasure was easily accessible by the Native Americans living on and around Mt. Nimham, being within a few miles of the mountain itself.

The Nochpeem, as with Native American Indians in general, felt it impossible to conceive of land ownership in the same terms as the Europeans who were to come. They felt they could no more own the land than they could the sun, the moon, or the stars. This basic misunderstanding between

Illustration 1: New York State Historical Marker for the Nochpeem Village near Boyd's Reservoir (*Photo by author*)

different cultures contributed to the eventual loss of the Nochpeem ancestral homeland to the European landowners and settlers.

Eastern Native American Indian culture and spirituality includes the concept of a special ceremony in which a young man (and some older men as well) would brave the elements to gain physical and spiritual strength. This was known as "beseachment of the elements" (Tarbox). Mt. Nimham was a spiritual center where many Native American Indians underwent their cleansing experience. Native Americans from near and far still return to this holy promenade to spiritually refresh themselves.

Like other tribes in the region, the Nochpeem relied heavily on an agriculture of corn, beans, and squash. They would perform a controlled burn of an area to clear it for planting and to create open fields to attract wildlife for hunting. They practiced field rotation as necessary to ensure the continued fertility of a planting field. Their diet was supplemented by fishing in the spring and summer, and hunting during the colder months. They hunted first with spears, and then gradually developed more efficient means, eventually using the bow and arrow for tracking deer, turkey, and the other plentiful wildlife (Murray and Osborn, 17).

Physically, the Wappinger were relatively tall and muscular, with many reaching over six feet in height. They used ceremonial painting and scarring to decorate their bodies.

According to historian Robert S. Grumet, these original New Yorkers were a social lot, frequently visiting relatives and friends, and trading with neighbors, in a constant stream of motion. They traveled via footpaths, some of which became roads during the colonial period, or paddled in their dugout canoes. They spent most of their time out-of-doors, often bare-chested. In colder weather, during the prime hunting season, large fur wraps provided a drafty sort of warmth. They rubbed their bodies with fish oil, bear grease or mud to ward off the chill of winter as well as the insects of summer.

These Native peoples passed down the contents of treaties and other agreements, without writing them down, through the generations. During these negotiations, they would hold a different shell as a memory marker in their hand as each article was discussed. At the conclusion of the agreement, they would recount the meaning of each marker. Then they would call the children together, instructing them to remember the details of each marker. Finally, the shells were then bound together on a string, and placed in a bag which was hung in the house of the sachem.

The youngsters were then warned to preserve this memory faithfully, so that they would not become treaty-breakers, which was considered an "abomination" to the Native people (Grumet).

Evidence of Nochpeem settlements on Mt. Nimham have come from eyewitness reports of the descendants of the Townsend and Smalley families. With its close proximity to Hawk Rock and Whang Hollow, this area would have been a prime hunting ground for the Nochpeem and their predecessors for thousands of years before the arrival of the Europeans. It has been reported that both Gipsy Trail Road and Coles Mills Road were originally Native trails.

It is believed that there are several burial grounds located on the mountain itself. In addition, at least four Native American Indian burial grounds are believed to exist within the valley to the east of the mountain known as "Whang Hollow." One is reportedly located near Little Buck Mountain. Another is described as being located on the farm which was situated on the northeastern corner of the intersection of Nichols Street and Horsepound Road. Additional potential burial grounds have been identified and are currently under investigation. The Native people were typically buried with their favorite utensils and weapons, facing eastward.

But life for the Native American Indian population would change forever with the introduction of the Europeans, or "Swannekins" ("salt water people") (Sultzman). While he was exploring the coast of North America for France in 1524, Giovanni da Verrazano discovered the narrow entrance to New York Harbor which today bears his name. His encounters with the native peoples at the mouth of the Hudson River were generally friendly, but unfortunately, he set the pattern for what was to follow by trying to kidnap some of them before his departure. During the next 80 years, this kind of "unofficial" contact continued as Spanish treasure fleets and English pirates passed through, riding the Gulf Stream home to Europe from the Caribbean. The Wappinger and other coastal tribes soon learned to be wary of the Swannekins who came ashore from the big ships to kidnap them and steal their food (Sultzman).

Chapter 2

Mount Nimham in the 17th Century

Having lived and prospered in their ancestral homeland for thousands of years, the 17th century would bring devastating changes for the Nochpeem people. European exploration brought forth an influx of fur traders, alcohol, war, and diseases for which the Nochpeem had no natural immunities. Every epidemic and each war that they were either forced into against the Europeans, or persuaded by the Europeans to engage in on their behalf, would serve to systematically weaken the Nochpeem and their Wappinger brethren. A clash of cultures would result in misunderstandings regarding land sales and accepted forms of justice. The Wappinger were also the victims of fraudulent deeds crafted by the wealthy elitists, which were rubber-stamped by a system of justice dominated by these same land barons. The Nochpeem, who believed the Great Spirit inhabited all that could be seen and unseen, thought it was no more possible to own the land as it was to own the stars, the sun, and the moon. They believed they had a right to use the land, and in some cases granted those same privileges to the Europeans. The Europeans, however, believed in total and exclusive rights of ownership. Based on these extreme cultural differences, conflict between these two peoples became the spirit of the times . . .

1609: On September 9th, Henry Hudson, captain of the ship *Half Moon*, while searching for the fabled Northwest Passage, entered the mouth of what was originally called the Mahikanittuk ("river that flows two ways") by the Wappinger, and later the "North River" by the early Europeans, which would eventually become known as the Hudson River, beginning the influx of Dutch fur traders into this area. Hudson dropped anchor near the north end of Manhattan Island and lowered his longboats to explore the area. His men were already nervous from a previous encounter with the Navasink, a Delaware tribe, near Sandy Hook. One of the boats became lost in a fog bank near Hellgate. When the fog parted, the crew suddenly found themselves being approached by a group of curious Wappinger in canoes, and the sailors apparently fired first. A barrage of arrows killed one sailor and wounded two others. Fortunately, the Wappinger withdrew, and the survivors were able to make their way back to the ship. Despite this initial hostile encounter, Hudson was able to entice a delegation of Wappinger sachems aboard his ship. Food and drink were served, and gifts exchanged, but the meetings remained uncomfortable, giving Hudson the feeling that he "durst not trust them." It would appear that the Wappinger "durst not trust Hudson" either, since he attempted to detain two of their young men as "guides" before raising anchor and continuing upriver. Once clear of the Wappinger, the people became friendlier further north of the Highlands, and the Munsee near Kingston deliberately broke their bows and arrows as a sign of their peaceful intentions (Sultzman).

On September 18th, Hudson was finally halted by shallow water at the Mahican villages just south of Albany. The Mahican were not only friendly, but were eager to trade. However, the fur trade aggravated a pre-existing rivalry between the Mahican and the Mohawk of the Iroquois League.

Although Hudson did not find the Northwest Passage he was searching for, the furs he brought back to Europe began an influx of Dutch traders into this area in the following year. The fur traders engaged the Native population in obtaining furs on their behalf by providing them with guns, knives and alcohol. This created an imbalance of power between the tribes, and soon the tribes were encroaching upon their neighbors' traditional territories, leading to an increase in intertribal warfare. And with this increased exposure to the Europeans, the Wappinger tribes were also subjected to diseases such as smallpox, measles and typhus which, by 1700, reduced the population to only about 10% of their original numbers. The original population numbered approximately 8,000, spread across seven tribes and about 30 villages (Sultzman).

However, the population may have been much larger than originally reported. This is because the Native population was actually subjected to the European diseases even before Hudson's arrival in this region. The Native populations along the northeastern U.S. seaboard had been exposed to these ailments by Giovanni da Verrazano's crew in 1524, and by the European fisherman along the New England coast who preceded the Pilgrims and Hudson. These diseases were then spread far and wide, as the Native peoples traded with each other throughout the northeast. So it is quite possible that Sultzman's figures actually reflected the post-exposure effects upon the Native people.

1626: Pieter Minuit, the newly appointed Director of New Netherlands, purchased Manhattan Island from the Metoac tribe for goods valued at $25. Fort Amsterdam was built with the settlement of New Amsterdam for the farmers to raise the food for its garrison. Dutch settlement soon spread across the lower Hudson Valley. Unlike the friendly relations the Dutch enjoyed with the Mahican, conflict with the Wappinger and neighboring tribes was immediate. A seemingly unimportant incident occurred in 1626 when a Wecquaesgeek man visiting Manhattan was robbed and murdered. His young nephew who accompanied him managed to escape unharmed, which years later would have serious consequences for the Dutch and the Wappinger.

1633-1635: A smallpox epidemic struck the Wappinger Confederacy, resulting in another devastating reduction of the local Native American population (Sultzman). In some cases, entire villages were wiped out as the Native population had no natural immunity to the European diseases.

As the fur trade grew, the supply of animals available for trapping and hunting was seriously depleted. So the Dutch increasingly began turning toward agricultural settlement instead. This gave rise to what would be the growing conflict between whites and the Native population over land, forcing the indigenous population out of their ancestral homelands.

1637: After Puritan settlers from Massachusetts spread out into the Connecticut River area (Windsor, Hartford and Wethersfield), tensions rose between the Pequots, the settlers and the Narragansetts. These tensions escalated into the first major war with the Native Americans, known as the Pequot War. Following a series of skirmishes and killings perpetrated by both sides, on May 26, 1637, nearly 300 Pequot men, women and children were burned out of their village, hunted down and massacred by an expedition led by John Underhill and John Mason of the Massachusetts Bay Colony. The war officially ended in September 1638, when the surviving Pequots were forced to sign the Treaty of Hartford.

1639: Tensions between the Native people and the Europeans escalated with the appointment of Director Kieft as Governor of New Amsterdam, an aggressive and extremely ignorant man inclined to run roughshod over the rights of the resident tribes. Kieft arrived just after the English had destroyed the Pequot (Pequot War, 1637), and English settlement had spread down the coast of western Connecticut to within a few miles of Fort Amsterdam.

1643-1645: The relatively unimportant incident of 1626, in which a Wecquaesgeek visiting Manhattan was robbed and murdered, resulted in the Wappinger War of 1643, which is more accurately known as Governor Kieft's War. The young nephew who accompanied him managed to escape unharmed, which years later would have serious consequences for the Dutch and the Wappinger people. One source of conflict was that Dutch farmers allowed their cows and pigs to wander freely in the woods, which often resulted in their invasion of the tribal corn fields. Not only did this bring immediate revenge on the offending animal, but the natives did not yet understand the European concept of the ownership of domestic animals, and a pig roaming loose in the woods was often viewed as fair game. After some pigs were 'stolen' at the De Vries plantation on Staten Island in 1640, Kieft dispatched 100 men to punish the Raritan (Unami Delaware) thought to be responsible. The Dutch killed several of them, took one chief prisoner, and mutilated the corpse of another. Raritan retaliation in the "Pig War" resulted in the killing of four of De Vries' workers and the burning of his farm. Kieft then ordered a war of extermination against the Raritan and offered a bounty of ten fathoms of wampum for every Raritan head brought to Fort Amsterdam.

The growing tension could have ended there. Unfortunately, the Wecquaesgeek nephew, in the custom of his people, chose this moment to take revenge for his uncle's murder in 1626 by killing a hapless Dutchman with his own axe. Not understanding the Native tradition of a blood debt, Kieft demanded the Wecquaesgeek surrender the murderer, but this request was refused. In March of 1642, Kieft dispatched a punitive expedition of 80 men under Ensign Hendrick Van Dyke to attack the Wecquaesgeek village at Yonkers. Fortunately, Van Dyke and his men got lost en route to the village. The Wecquaesgeek, however, soon learned of this attempt to attack them and, becoming alarmed, immediately signed a peace agreement with the Dutch. However, by this time the nephew had found refuge with another tribe, and the Dutch never got their hands on him.

A similar situation developed after a group of Dutchmen used alcohol to their advantage by serving it in excess to the son of a Hackensack (Unami Delaware) sachem, and then robbed him of his beaver coat. In what has been called the "Whiskey War," he retaliated by shooting a Dutchman and then fled to the Tankiteke. The peace which ended the war between the Mohawk and Mahican in 1628 had also bound them together as allies against the Algonquin, Montagnais, and Huron, who had driven the Iroquois from the St. Lawrence River in 1610.

To preserve their security, the Dutch did not provide firearms to the tribes near their settlements in the lower Hudson Valley. Sensing their increasing disadvantage, this refusal added to the growing resentment by the Wappinger, Munsee, Unami, and Metoac. To acquire even more guns, both the Mohawk and Mahican needed more furs and hunting territory. This was especially true for the Mahican, since they had been forced east of the Hudson by their defeat in 1628 at the hands of the Mohawk. They expanded north, east and south, the last direction being mostly at the expense of the Wappinger. The Wecquaesgeek fled south to what they thought was the safety of the Dutch settlements on Manhattan. They remained nearby for two weeks before moving across the river to the Tappan and Hackensack villages at Pavonia (Jersey City).

Ignoring the advice of his own Council, Kieft decided to exterminate the Wecquaesgeek (known as the "Wickerscreek" to the settlers) and set an example to the other "wilden" ("wild men") in the vicinity. In what has become known as the Pavonia Massacre, he ordered a surprise attack to be made on the night of February 23, 1643. Maryn Andriansen was sent with a group of militia to Corlear's Hook, while Sergeant Rodolf and his soldiers from Fort Amsterdam were to attack the village at Pavonia. Kieft's orders were to kill all of the warriors and take the women and children prisoner, to be used as slaves. Only Andriansen followed these instructions. Rodolf and his men just slaughtered every Wecquaesgeek in the sleeping village at Pavonia without regard for age or gender. The killing by these Dutch "Christians" was especially brutal, including the hacking to death of babies in their mothers' arms, in addition to torture and mutilation. This episode represented one of the most horrendous events in the history of Native and European relations.

Kieft expected some retaliation, but under-estimated the extent of the ill-feeling among the tribes of the area against the Dutch. As news of the massacre spread, the other Wappinger raided the outlying European farms and settlements. It was during this time that the infamous killing of Anne Hutchinson, of the Eastchester-Pelham Bay area, and the other members of her settlement by the Wecquaesgeek and Siwanoy took place. Her sister settlement, located a bit to the south, and headed by John Throckmorton, included the ancestors of this author. Richard Maxson, the settlement's blacksmith, and his son, Richard Jr., were also killed on August 20th, 1643, by the Wecquaesgeek and Siwanoy in the area now known as "Throg's Neck" (originally named for Throckmorton).

Governor Kieft's War quickly spread to at least 20 tribes from New Jersey to northern New York, including the Nochpeem. The Nochpeem were charged with the holding of Dutch prisoners seized from their ships on the North River, " . . . *and subsequently the Indian fortresses of the Highlands became the receptacle of Dutch prisoners"* (Ruttenber, 64). With only 250 men, the Dutch were nearly overwhelmed. After concluding a treaty with the Mahican and Mohawk, Kieft then offered 25,000 guilders to the English in Connecticut for 150 men to help put down the uprising. Dutch and English forces, with the aid of the Mahicans, combined with terrible effect during 1644 and 1645 to crush the Wappinger and their allies, thus turning the tide against them. In the winter of 1644, the Englishman John Underhill led an expedition in the slaughter of between 500 to 700 Siwanoys and Tankitekes at the village of Nanichiestawack ("place of safety") in what is now the Pound Ridge-Bedford area, including Wappinger Chief Katonah. The Native people had gathered for a corn festival, with many women and children in attendance, and Underhill saw this as his chance to inflict the greatest harm possible. The women and children were herded into their lodges, which were then torched. As the women and children were being burned alive, they did not cry out or scream, according to the Dutch eyewitness accounts. By the summer of 1645, more than 2,600 Native Americans had been killed, about 1,600 being from the Wappinger Confederacy, until the Wappinger finally asked the Mahican to mediate a peace for them with the Dutch (Sultzman).

In the period following Governor Kieft's War, Dutch settlement in New Netherlands increased from 2,000 in 1648 to more than 10,000 by 1660. Beginning in 1652, it had spread north into the Munsee country in the Esopus Valley near present-day Kingston. During 1659 this erupted into a series of conflicts known as the Esopus Wars (1659-1664).

According to Ruttenber, in early April of 1644, Chief Pappenoharrow (then chief of the Nochpeem) came to Fort Amsterdam, and pledged that they *"would not henceforth commit any injury whatever on the inhabitants of New Amsterdam, their cattle and houses."*

1655: Following the disastrous war against the Wappinger between 1643 and 1645, the Wappinger tried to peacefully coexist with the Dutch. But in September of 1655, a Dutch farmer on Manhattan named Van Dyke shot and killed a Wappinger woman when he caught her "borrowing" a peach from a tree in his garden. This resulted in the Wappinger sending canoes with more than 200 warriors down the Hudson to Manhattan to kill Van Dyke. Eventually they found him and put an arrow into him, only wounding him, but while searching for him they engaged in a fight with burgher guards (Dutch militia). The warriors retreated across the river to reorganize and continue their complaint by burning Dutch farms at Pavonia, Hoboken, and Staten Island. At least 50 Dutch were killed in the fighting, which became known as the "Peach War" (Sultzman).

1656: A second devastating smallpox epidemic swept through the Hudson Valley, taking the lives of many of the most susceptible, including the very young and very old members of the local tribes.

1663: During the Second Esopus War, Lieutenant Wolfertse Van Couwenhoven of the West India Company was assigned command of the company's river yacht. He passed extensive time with the neutral Wappinger people, and persuaded one of their sachems to undertake a mission to obtain the release of some white captives, which was successfully accomplished. During this time, he fathered a son named Kowehahum, who became a leading member of the tribe. Forty years later Kowehahum's signature would appear on an Indian land deed (MacCracken, 267). The Second Esopus War pitted the Mahicans against the Mohawks.

1664: In September, the British fleet captured New Amsterdam without firing a shot, and the dominant role of the Dutch in North America ended. Despite this, few of the Dutch settlers left the area. However, now a steady influx of English colonists began to arrive. But few were willing to settle up the river and challenge the Iroquois, so most of the new settlement occurred on the Wappinger and Munsee lands along the lower Hudson River Valley.

1675: Known as "King Philip's War", this intense conflict raged between New England tribes and English colonists in New England until 1676. Approximately 800 colonists and 3,000 Native Americans lost their lives, and more than half of the towns in New England faced attacks during the conflict. Even though the Wappinger and Nochpeem were not directly involved, it sent a chilling message to both the colonists and the Native people as to what could happen here in the Hudson Valley.

1687: Two Dutch traders (Jan Roelof Sybrandt and Lambert Dorland) claimed to have purchased a portion of what would become Putnam County, including Mt. Nimham, from the Nochpeem for a "competent" sum of money on October 26th. The property was described as *"a strip of land along the Hudson shore in the Highland, all the way from Anthony's Nose to Polipel Island, east into the woods to a marked tree"* (MacCracken, 52). No eastern boundary was clearly defined, and so the local governor did not grant a patent, instead awaiting a more detailed survey. This sale was later disputed by the Wappinger, who claimed that only the western one-fourth of Putnam County, consisting of approximately 15,000 acres, was sold to these traders (Pelletreau, 79).

1692: Another devastating smallpox epidemic struck the region, further reducing the population of the Wappinger tribes in the Hudson Valley (Sultzman). By this time the population of the local tribes had been decimated by the series of wars and epidemics occurring throughout the 1600s. And the drastic reductions of the animal population, required to meet the demand of the fur traders, caused starvation for the Native American Indians who relied on their meat for food. The beaver was most highly prized, for not only food and clothing, but for the oils obtained and used in their medicinal remedies (Ruttenber, 24). By 1700, according to Robert Grumet, there were scarcely more than 3,000 Native American Indians living in the Lower Hudson Valley.

1697: The Dutch fur traders Sybrandt and Dorland sold the property they claimed to have purchased from the Nochpeem to Adolph Philipse, a wealthy merchant, on June 16th. On June 17th, Philipse obtained a royal patent from the English Crown for land extending all the way from the Hudson River to the Connecticut border, an area to be known as the Upper Highland Patent of the Philipse Patent. But the original deed of sale never defined the eastern boundary, which was yet further extended by the Philipses to reach all the way to the Connecticut border. The Philipses never recorded this new deed, most likely realizing it would have been rejected as being invalid due to the ever changing eastern boundary, and because there was no additional compensation extended to the Nochpeem for the expanded boundary, which was a legal requirement for such an extension of land from the original deed.

As to why these land patents were so easily procured from the local authorities, the historian and former Philipstown Turnpike resident Philips Smith provided the following explanation: *"The fees incident to the procuration of a patent were important sources of revenue to the officers concerned. Only 1,000 acres could be granted to one person; but this rule was evaded by associating a number of merely nominal parties. And the officers through whose hands the papers were passed were often largely interested in the grants. In this respect the Colonial Government became exceedingly corrupt, and stood greatly in need of a reform like that wrought by the Revolution"* (41).

In summary, the Philipses' original purchase of approximately 15,000 acres was illegally expanded into a vast domain of over 205,000 acres (Grumet, 90).

The Wappinger people, systematically weakened by war, disease, and displacement, would continue their attempts to regain a part of their ancestral homeland over the next 80 years.

Chapter 3

Mount Nimham in the 18th Century

The early part of the 18th century would herald the birth of the great Sachem of the Wappinger people, the patriot Chief Daniel Nimham. Born into a time of great change and challenge for his people, this man who converted to Christianity would truly live his faith. This was consistently demonstrated by the charitable manner in which he would strive to protect and preserve that which remained of his ancestral homeland. The wealthy aristocratic patent holders, on the other hand, would go to great lengths to legitimize their illegal land grabs. Although their fraudulent deeds were clearly in violation of the laws in effect at that time, the courts would ignore legality in favor of cronyism. As tensions grew between the tenant farmers and the aristocrats, the seeds of discontent would be sown, leading to revolution and the birth of a new, great nation . . .

1700: Between 1667 and 1783 there were over 200 references made in colonial records to individuals identified by the name of "Nimham" (Grumet, 81). Some of these references point to a Native leader from Long Island, and later New Jersey, and finally the Hudson Valley. According to a history of early Dutchess County, Daniel Nimham (see Illustration 2) was born around the year 1700, though most historians now believe his birth date to have occurred around 1726 (Tarbox, 3; Smith, 175-176; Grumet, 87; Pritchard, 412), the son of One Shake and grandson of Old Man Nimham (Nimhammau). It has been reported that he was a contemporary of Catharyna Brett's three boys, Francis (1707-1787), Robert (b. 1711), and Rivery (dates unknown) (MacCracken, 68). Born at a time when white farmers and missionaries were moving into the Hudson Valley, the bright articulate youngster learned to speak and write English while growing up near the Brett family in the homeland of the Wiccopee, a sub-tribe of the Nochpeem, in the Fishkill and East Fishkill areas. In turn, he taught the Bretts the ways of the forest and the Native Americans. It was said he was a good and honest man, who could not be corrupted by money, goods, or alcohol (Grumet, 82).

1721: According to MacCracken, early records in Dutchess County indicate that "Young Nimham" was paid 12 shillings for bringing in two wolves' heads to the local authorities. Two other Natives, Pechewyn and Taquehamas, brought in 3 wolves' heads and were paid 5 shillings per head. The bounty on wolves continued until 1780 (267). It is most likely that "Young Nimham" as described here actually referred to Daniel's father, One Shake.

Illustration 2: Chief Daniel Nimham *(Sculpture and photo courtesy of Michael Keropian)*

Also in this year, Catharyna Brett filed a complaint with the governor, claiming that her *"surveyors had been obstructed and driven off by drunken Indians, and that on another occasion they had come to her house threatening to kill her."* It has been reported that she had received a prior warning of possible trouble from her old friend, Nimham, which ensured her safety during this encounter. This was the only act of violence by Native Americans ever reported in all of the history of Dutchess County (MacCracken, 270).

1726: Based upon a deposition provided by the patriot Daniel Nimham in the year 1762, in which he was described as being 36 years of age at that time, 1726 is often considered the most likely year of his birth (Grumet, 87). However, the exact year of his birth is still the subject of some debate, though most historians now agree that it occurred in the period between 1724 and 1726.

1730: In this year, it is reported that "King Nimham" was selected to testify in a lawsuit concerning the sovereignty of the "River Indians." He was identified as a "Sakemaker," which was how the old deeds referred to the Sachem of the tribe. In the deposition, it was stated that *"the Wappinger were the ancient inhabitants of the eastern shore of Hudson's River, from the city of New York to about the middle of Beekman's Patent."* It also noted that the Mahicans inhabited the lands north of the Wappinger, but that the two tribes constituted one nation (MacCracken, 268). Again, given the date, this was most likely the elder Nimham rather than Daniel himself.

Although they were often referred to as "River Indians," the Nochpeem's presence in the Highlands region also gave them the moniker of "Highland Indians."

It was also in this year that payment for the Nine Partners Patent in Dutchess County was finally made to the Mahican and Wappinger. "Nimham" was noted to have received goods in equal value to 150 English pounds. The elder Nimham accompanied the surveyor, George Clinton, to both protect them from wandering hunting parties and to ensure that the correct boundaries were recorded. MacCracken noted, *"As Clinton's sons were often with him, (the elder) Nimham may have known both James and George, leaders of New York in the Revolution"* (269).

1737: The Colonial Assembly designated the Upper Highland Patent of the Philipse Patent as the South Precinct of Dutchess County, and the Philipses began leasing land to immigrants from Massachusetts, Rhode Island, Connecticut, Long Island and lower Westchester.

1744: When King George's War (1744-1748) broke out between Britain and France, the Iroquois, except the Mohawk, chose to remain neutral. Likewise, the Wappinger and Mahican made a similar decision, but French allies from Canada raided settlements in Vermont, New Hampshire, and the Hudson Valley north of Albany. Fearful of impending attacks along the lower river, the colonists massacred several peaceful Munsee families near Walden, New York, during the fall of 1745. The Munsee and Wappinger immediately left the area and remained in Pennsylvania until 1746. That year, a French army of 960 men under Philippe de Vaudreuil captured Fort Massachusetts on the

Hoosic River, which spread fear throughout the lower Hudson Valley of an impending attack. So the fearful colonists sent word to the displaced Nochpeem and Wappinger in Pennsylvania, explaining that the incident at Walden the year before was a terrible mistake. The Wappinger and Mahican suddenly found they were welcome back in the Hudson Valley to defend it against the French, although the feared attack never materialized (Sultzman).

1745: The patriot Daniel Nimham was reportedly baptized in the Christian faith in this year. Catharyna Brett, a neighbor, landowner, and mill owner, was instrumental in his conversion (Murray and Osborn, 18). He took the biblical name of "Daniel," which would serve to be rather prophetic. According to the Bible, during the captivity of the Jews in Babylon, in the sixth century B.C., the prophet Daniel continued to pray to his God against the express command of the king. As a result, Daniel was thrown into a lions' den to be devoured. But God sent an angel to protect him, and he emerged miraculously unharmed the next day.

Like his biblical namesake, Daniel Nimham was born into a time of great change, challenge, and despair for his people.

1748: Elisha Cole Jr. (1719-1801), who was married to Hannah Smalley (d. 1811), built a grist mill at the base of the southernmost portion of Mt. Nimham. Elisha and Hannah had moved from Harwich, Massachusetts, to what is now known as Putnam County, during the fall of 1746 or spring of 1747. He built a log house near the stream that is the outlet of Barrett's Pond in the town of Kent. In 1748 he built a gristmill on the West Branch of the Croton River. Eventually, a carding mill and saw mill were added (see Illustration 3). This area became known as "Cole's Mills", and was owned and operated by various members of the Cole family until 1888, when New York City finalized the purchase of the water rights to construct the West Branch Reservoir. Elisha was a popular Baptist preacher, serving at the Mt. Carmel Baptist Church in the hamlet of Carmel, and was partially paralyzed. He and his wife had seven sons and five daughters; two of the sons and a son-in-law became preachers themselves, with another son serving as a deacon. The land where they settled in Kent was purchased from the Commissioners of Forfeiture after it had been confiscated from Roger and Mary Philipse Morris. Elisha and his sons were members of the 7th Regiment of the Dutchess County Militia, under Col. Henry Ludington, during the War of Independence (Cole Family Genealogy).

1749: Adolph Philipse died intestate in this year, and the Upper Highland Patent was passed on to his nephew, Frederick Philipse (Pelletreau, 28). Frederick Philipse passed away in 1751, leading to the division of the Upper

Highlands Patent of the Philipse Patent into nine separate lots.

COLES MILLS, 1.— House and mill over West Branch of Croton River.

Illustration 3: Coles Mills (*Courtesy of George C. Whipple, III*)

1750: Chief One Shake passed away in this year, and it is believed the patriot Daniel Nimham succeeded his father after 1752 as Sachem of the Wappinger and Nochpeem, which were the largest of the remaining tribes within the Wappinger Confederacy. These tribes were scattered in small villages across the Highlands in what is now known as Putnam County and the southern portion of Dutchess County. Chief Nimham was believed to have spent most of his time in the Wappinger village which was possibly located just southwest of where Wal-Mart and Sam's Club are now located in Fishkill. Others believe the village was found off of Route 52 in the Wiccopee, where Fishkill Creek and Sprout Brook converge (Tarbox, 3). He was also known to have lived for a time in the 1750s to 1770s in a Nochpeem settlement located at the northwest corner of what is now Boyd's Reservoir in Kent.

1754: After Frederick Philipse's death in 1751, the Upper Highland Patent of the Philipse Patent was surveyed and divided into nine lots granted to three heirs: Mary Philipse (who would later marry Col. Roger Morris of the British Army), Philip Philipse, and Susannah Philipse Robinson, who was married to Beverly Robinson. Mt. Nimham was included in Lot No. 5, which was owned by Mary Philipse (Pelletreau, 17).

1755-1763: Sir William Johnson, the English Crown's Indian agent, knowing of the bravery of the Wappinger, asked the patriot Chief Daniel Nimham to support England's war with France in the New World, called the Seven Years War, but more popularly known as the French and Indian War (which was actually the fourth such conflict between the English and French in the New World). Nimham and his band of 300 warriors ended up protecting the very patent holders who had confiscated the Wappingers' ancestral homeland. While the Wappinger men were fighting in Canada in support of the British, colonial authorities, under the urging of the Philipses, moved the remaining Wappinger, mainly women, children, and the elderly, to the Christian Indian mission settlement at Stockbridge, Massachusetts, for the duration of the war. There, the Wappinger lived within a six-square mile mission that was established in 1736 for the converted Native American population, along a bend in the Housatonic River (Grumet, 88).

While claiming that this move was made for the protection of the Wappinger, the Philipses then hurriedly worked to recruit additional settlers to move on to the Wappinger ancestral homeland. These tenant farmers often reused previous Native settlements for the placement of their farms. Native trails were reused as roadways by the new entrants.

According to MacCracken, it was Nimham who brought his people to Stockbridge. MacCracken believed that Nimham was very familiar with Stockbridge, possibly having gone to school there at one time. While Nimham was said to be there, the famous theologian and philosopher Jonathan Edwards was also visiting the area.

Nimham and his brothers fought bravely alongside Rogers' Rangers during the French and Indian War. Upon returning from the conflict, the Wappinger found their remaining ancestral lands settled, and in effect, confiscated. For the next 15 years, Nimham traveled from village to village in Dutchess and what is now Putnam County. It is reported that every year, on the anniversary of his birth, he would climb to the top of Mt. Nimham to meditate and proclaim all the land he could see as the Wappingers' rightful ancestral homeland. The settlement where he often stayed was located near what is now the area west of Boyd's Dam, at the southwest base of the mountain, along what is now Route 301, in the town of Kent (Murray and Osborn).

1758: Mary Philipse, owner of Lot No. 5 of the Philipse Patent (which is now the central section of Kent, including western Whang Hollow and Mt. Nimham), married Col. Roger Morris of the British Army (Pelletreau, 87).

During the summer of 1757, frontier settlements in Orange and Dutchess

Counties (including what is now Putnam County) were attacked by Munsee warriors angry over being cheated out of their lands. The following year, the New York Colonial Legislature responded by confiscating all of the remaining native lands in the lower Hudson Valley. White settlers immediately began moving into the abandoned lands, including the Smalley, Townsend and Russell families into the Mt. Nimham area. When the Moravian missionaries protested, they were arrested as French agents and banished from New York. These missionaries not only exposed the traders who were illegally selling alcohol to the Native American Indians, but also provided legal advice which kept some Natives from being cheated. Rather than supporting these efforts, many whites resented the missionaries' interference with "nature taking its course." This was especially true of the Moravians, who in 1740 established a mission at Shekomeko (Pine Plains) for the Wappinger and Mahican still living along the river.

On March 13th, the patriot Chief Daniel Nimham was elected as the Constable for the Town of Stockbridge (Grumet, 89). But although he owned land there, it was reported that he continued to move back and forth to the Wiccopee, his ancestral homeland.

On July 3rd, Daniel Nimham was given power of attorney by his people to act on behalf of the Wappinger in their dealings with the local officials, landowners, and tenant farmers. This authority was granted by fellow Wappinger leaders named Hendrick Wauman, Arie Sawck, Out Quamos, and John Backto. In separate letters, he also received power of attorney from his friends Mektoos, One Pound Pactone, and Stephen Cowenhum. Nimham received legal guidance from Samuel Munroe of Beekman, who was reported to be the grandson of one William Munroe, a tough Scot who had been captured by Oliver Cromwell at the Battle of Worcester. The elder Munroe was deported from his native land, along with thousands of other Scots, to be sold into slavery at Boston (MacCracken, 274).

The patriot Chief Daniel Nimham would spend the rest of his life fighting to regain the ancestral homeland of the Wappinger. By this period of time, the Wappinger had already lost 90% of their lands and their population (Grumet, 81).

1760: When the Wappinger returned from the French and Indian War, they found that what little remained of their hunting land was endangered by suits arising from "the Gore dispute." The Philipses, not content with the 200,000-plus acres of land they already controlled under dubious title, had also laid claim to land in the Fishkill and East Fishkill area. Included in the disputed lands was the principal Native village at Wiccopee. This greatly angered the

Wappinger, who then decided to engage in private sales and leases to the newly-arrived tenant farmers. These transactions became known as "Indian deeds" (MacCracken, 272).

One of the most prominent families of Mt. Nimham arrived here around the year 1760. James Smalley, reportedly from Cape Cod, Massachusetts, settled on the mountain which would eventually bear his family name during the better part of the 19th century (Blake, 328).

1761: In December of this year, King George III issued a proclamation, which was re-issued by Lt. Gov. Colden of the New York colony on February 17, 1762. It required *"persons having seated themselves on land claimed by Indians to remove therefrom on pain of being prosecuted with the utmost rigor of the law."* Officials were forbidden to possess any land claimed by the Native Americans, without proper license from the lawful authority. But even this proclamation from the King did not stop the wealthy landlords in Dutchess County, which included what is now Putnam County, from usurping the rights of the Native people (MacCracken, 281).

1762: Following the proclamations issued in 1761 and 1762 protecting Native land claims, the New York Council was informed on July 28th that *"Daniel Nimham, an Indian, claims lands in Dutchess County in possession of Col. Frederick Philipse's heirs, and of Mr. Brett"* (MacCracken, 277).

1763: Lt. Governor Colden counted 432 members of the Wappinger tribes, scattered about the area between Westchester and Southern Dutchess Counties. This was down from the last count which had been made in the year 1700, which then totaled approximately 1,000 members.

The "melting away" of the Wappinger population in the lower Hudson is a perfect example of what happened to most of the eastern tribes when confronted with the "advance of civilization." The blame cannot easily be attributed to any single reason. Although illegal, alcohol contributed to social disintegration and greased the wheels of a series of suspicious land sales to whites that usually left the Wappinger with little beyond the clothes on their backs. The wars of the 1600s and 1700s had also weakened the Wappinger. Epidemics accelerated the process by killing off both the young and the old. Smallpox epidemics had struck in the Hudson Valley during 1636, 1656, and 1692 followed by the scourge of malaria after 1700 (Sultzman).

1764: As the Philipses continued to lease disputed lands to the new entrants coming into the area, Nimham decided to proceed with the sale of deeds to lands of dubious title to some of these tenant farmers. These were known as

"Indian deeds." Many tenant farmers, unhappy with the high rents charged by the Philipses, began dealing directly with the Wappinger instead. One document of sale, dated July 24, 1764, granted land to Nathaniel Worder in Beekman, property which extended to "Whalley Pond" (sp). The sale also called for a yearly rent of *"two peppercorns in and upon the feast of St. Michael the Archangel"* (MacCracken, 276).

Chief Nimham then escalated his attempts to collect on the sale of the Indian deeds. On September 18th he sued Philip Griffith for 50 pounds, and on September 19th he sued Isaac Chase for payment of 10 pounds. On November 6th, the Wappinger affirmed their choice of Samuel Munroe as their attorney and guardian. This was acknowledged before Judge Jacobus Ter Boss of the Court of Common Pleas in Poughkeepsie.

1765: Based upon the claim originally filed in 1762, on March 6th a hearing was granted in New York City by the New York Common Council. The claim was filed by Nimham against three of the great Hudson Valley area land owners: Mary Philipse Morris and her husband, Col. Roger Morris, Beverly Robinson, and Philip Philipse, to recover 204,800 acres of their land (most of what is now Putnam County). This also covered the Philipse-Morris property in Lot No. 5, which included the Mt. Nimham area.

The plaintiffs demonstrated that the original purchase by Sybrandt and Dorland (1687-1691), though licensed for purchase, had never been consummated. They argued that the original survey was incomplete, stating that the property extended eastward to a marked tree along the Rombout-Philipse line, with no western or southern line being defined. Without definitive borders, the deed would never have been deemed as being legal. In addition, when Adolph Philipse bought the property from them in 1697, the new deed described the land differently, and was therefore highly questionable. Philipse's deed extended the land to the entire length of the Rombout Patent, 16 miles further than the previous deed.

Then, Governor Fletcher, in granting the Patent, and without warrant, extended the deed even further, all the way to Connecticut (an additional four miles). But no additional payment was made for either extension of land, nor was the original purchase price listed. The attorneys for the Wappinger claimed that therefore, under the King's proclamation of 1761, the Wappinger people were entitled to the deeded land.

Just as the Philipses were about to lose the case, Beverly Robinson, the husband of Susannah Philipse, suddenly reached into his pocket and produced another deed dated August 13, 1702, which included all the lands in question. This deed was supposedly signed by several members of the Wappinger. However, this deed had never been recorded, which alone should have made it void based on precedents in previous land disputes at that time (a similar case involving Arnout Viele, who also had not recorded his own deed, had resulted in Viele losing his land). In addition, the Wappinger disputed the signatories on the deed, saying that the entire Council was required to approve the sale in order for it to be valid. No one had ever previously seen this deed before Robinson pulled it out of his pocket, just as he and the Philipses were about to lose their claims.

Apparently, Robinson and his Philipse in-laws had previously learned that William Penn's heirs had successfully used this same tactic in dispossessing the Minisink tribe of their lands in Pennsylvania in 1737. So they employed the same ruse of producing an unknown, unlicensed, and unregistered deed to steal the Wappinger homeland (Grumet, 90).

Unfortunately, those sitting in judgment on the Common Council were themselves "gentlemen of estates," who had much to lose personally if they voted in favor of Nimham. The number of Philipse tenants who had turned to Indian deeds had grown so large as to create a real threat to the status quo. The acceptance of these Indian deeds could have had catastrophic impacts on their own land holdings. So instead, the Council ignored the law, ignored the rules and regulations regarding the filing of deeds, ignored the content requirements needed for a valid deed, and ignored the previous legal precedents, and ruled in favor of the Philipses.

To add insult to injury, Samuel Munroe was then arrested by the Attorney General and imprisoned on a charge of "maintenance." This was a legal term of that time used to describe *"interference in a suit in which the offender has no interest."* This, of course, was ludicrous given that Munroe was the officially designated attorney and guardian of the Wappinger.

Following up on this victory, Beverly Robinson then began evicting tenants who had withheld payment of rents to the Philipses while honoring Indian deeds. This added to the growing resentment between the tenants and the aristocratic patent holders. By the middle of the fall, groups of tenant farmers were meeting in the Patterson-Towners area (Morrison's Tavern and Samuel Towner's) to plan their grievances. William Prendergast of Quaker Hill and John Kane of Pawling emerged as the leaders of this movement (MacCracken, 301). In November, two regiments of regular British troops were sent from Poughkeepsie, along with 200 more troops from New York City. They were armed with muskets and canons and were sent to put down attempts by the local patriots to stop the British land encroachment. For the first time, British troops fired upon American patriots in a bloody struggle which lasted from November of 1765 until July of 1766. This became known as the "Settler's Revolt." News of the conflict appeared in Massachusetts newspapers and stirred a response which helped give birth to the Sons of Liberty, the precursor organization of the patriotic cause during the American Revolution. Beverly Robinson, whose fraudulent deed had denied justice to the Wappinger, along with Oliver Delancey, led the attack to depose the patriots in colonial Fredericksburg, and would later serve the loyalists, when the Revolution spread to include all the colonies.

1766: Unable to gain any justice in the colonial courts, the patriot Chief Daniel Nimham, along with six Mahican men and women, William Gregg, Jr., and two interpreters, sailed to England to petition King George III (Vaughan, 177). Gregg served as the benefactor of the group, in exchange for land provided by the Indians. From the time of his landing in Britain until his return to New York, Nimham was the guest of His Majesty King George III. A private audience was granted with the King's representative, and the Native visitors were decked out in lace coats, silk ribbands, and hats, along with silver armbands and buckskin moccasins. Even though other Native American Indians had appeared in the King's Court before, Nimham and his band greatly impressed the royals with their command of the English language. But because they had arrived in England without the prior consent of the King, and without a letter of introduction from any of the New World Governors, protocol demanded that the King not take any direct action in response to their claims (MacCracken, 289). Instead, their issues were presented to the Lords of Trade on August 30th. But it has been reported that the King was personally impressed by the Wappinger claims, and was somewhat sympathetic to their plight. The Lords of Trade were also impressed by Nimham's claims as well.

Nimham and his comrades left England near the end of September, returning to New York in late October. Upon his return, Chief Daniel Nimham presented a new petition to Sir Harry Moore, the Governor of New York, in yet another attempt to regain the Wappinger ancestral homeland.

Following their meeting with the Lords of Trade, the Secretary of State, the Earl of Shelburne, on behalf of the King, wrote to Governor Harry Moore of New York, *"the small and inadequate consideration usually given on occasion of those purchases and the arts and management by which they have generally been acquired seldom entitle these claimants to an equitable relief."* He asked Moore to *"take under your most serious consideration the case of these distressed people and turn your thoughts to every possible measure that may obtain for them a just and lasting satisfaction and that you will take on yourself as far as justice and the reason of the thing shall demand the office of their advocate and protector.*" Sir William Johnson, the Chief of Indian Affairs, was thus charged with the responsibility of looking into the Wappinger claims and acting as "their advocate and protector."

The Earl of Shelburne also wrote to Johnson directly, asking him to review the Wappinger claims. But Johnson, who had greatly benefited by the Wappinger participation in the French and Indian War on behalf of the King, felt he could not seek justice for them, because doing so would, in his mind, unravel the very fabric of the new state. He was not about to compromise his position and good standing with the Council members in the New World, from whom he owed his position (MacCracken, 291).

The previous spring, Prendergast and his fellow dissatisfied tenant farmers from Fredericksburgh marched to New York City to rescue two tenants from Westchester County who were being evicted from their land. At the same time, protests had grown throughout the Hudson Valley against the Philipses and Van Cortlandts. Governor Moore called out the militia to disperse the angry crowd. Beverly Robinson personally took charge of the 200 British troops and militia to subdue the rebels. It was reported that on a Sabbath Day, the rebel houses were burned, while others were pillaged and plundered. With the Settler's Revolt, the animosity between the tenant farmers had reached a boiling point which was to foretell the coming break between the Crown and the colonists.

And thus, the seeds of revolution were sown.

1767: Following Nimham's presentation of a new petition the previous fall, a second hearing took place in Poughkeepsie on March 1st, with the trial set for March 6th, and representing Nimham and the Wappinger was the legal team of Asa Spalding and Cyrus Marsh from Connecticut. The plaintiffs brought in tenants of the Philipses to provide testimony, which took a great deal of courage in the aftermath of the Settler's Revolt. They all spoke of being told by the Philipses when they first moved to these lands that they must also settle with the Native American Indians who occupied the land. Daniel Townsend spoke of when he arrived in these lands in 1738 that he had to come to agreement with the Native American Indians before they would let him live there. David Austin deposed that in 1730 he had a dispute with the local Natives which resulted in their burning his hay stacks. When he complained to Adolph Philipse, he was told that the area was considered to be the Indians' hunting grounds, and that he must come to agreement with them. James Philips likewise reported that he found a wigwam on his land, and was forced to come to terms with the locals in yet another instance.

These events indicated that the Philipses themselves had acknowledged the ultimate land ownership rights of the Wappinger people. Asa Spalding, Nimham's attorney, concluded that *"clouds of witnesses have been adduced, whereby methinks it hath been fully, clearly, and absolutely proved, that almost every Person that ever settled himself upon said Lands before 1756 did it only by permission of Said Tribe"* (MacCracken, 295).

In his final summation, Spalding reiterated that the Wappingers' land had never been purchased. He asked, if land could be transferred without purchase, why not any man's land? He stated further that the Indians were still a nation, with a valid treaty in existence with the King of England. The fact that the Philipses had not used the land for so many years proved that they had no title to it. The experts all agreed that it took a concourse of Indians to agree to a valid sale. And the fact that Beverly Robinson's 1702 deed had never been executed in New York, and had never been acknowledged before any recognized legal authority, violated English law. Spalding also raised the fact that witnesses had heard both Adolph and Frederick Philipse themselves say that they had not purchased the land.

The Philipses' attorney, John Morin Scott, choosing to ignore the inconvenient legalities of the case, instead focused on the possible impact of the patentees losing their property rights, including those sitting on the Council.

Scott's strategy worked, as the predominant influence of the wealthy landowners over the Council made it impossible for Nimham and the Wappinger to gain a favorable ruling. On March 17th and 26th, the verdict was published in the *New York Post Boy*: The Indians had no title whatever to any of the land. They ruled that the August 13, 1702 deed, conveniently produced by Beverly Robinson at the very last moments of the previous trial, was valid. They proclaimed that Beverly Robinson was *"a man of Character, of Prudence, and of undoubted Loyalty"* (MacCracken, 299).

That spelled the end for the Indian deeds and any further legal claims by the People of Manitou (Pritchard). It was then reported that they returned to Stockbridge and began to scatter. Chief Daniel Nimham sold his lot at Stockbridge and resumed his commutation from village to village between the Housatonic and Hudson Rivers (Grumet, 90). One such village included the settlement located west of Boyd's Dam, along the southwestern base of Mt. Nimham. The Chief had now become a wanderer in his own homeland.

1775: The patriot Chief Daniel Nimham traveled to Boston and addressed the newly-formed Continental Congress. He pledged himself to the cause of freedom, hoping to gain some relief from the Crown's patent holders who still held possession of his tribal homeland. His son, the patriot Abraham Nimham, joined the Massachusetts militia and was awarded the rank of captain. Nimham joined his son at the Battle of Bunker Hill (which actually occurred on Breed's Hill), along with Major General Israel Putnam. They later served with Washington's army at Valley Forge, and at the Battle of Monmouth, which was the largest land battle of the American Revolution. At Valley Forge, Seneca women brought food to help feed the starving Continental Army (Tarbox, 5).

According to Pelletreau's account in 1886, *"In the Revolution, Nimham and his warriors took an active part. Some sixty of them, expert marksmen and skilled in war, joined the American forces and fought with a bravery and valor worthy of their ancient race, in the days of their glory"* (84).

Just after British troops fired upon the patriots at Concord on April 18, 1775, the inhabitants of New York called for regional meetings in each County of all who were opposed to the oppressive acts of the English Parliament. It was decided that a "Pledge" (see Appendix A) was needed to determine which side each colonist supported. As the historian William Blake so poignantly described in his 1849 "History of Putnam County":

"Between submission and resistance they were called to choose; the former they had yielded to until it had ceased to become a virtue, and the latter was the only alternative left to men who were determined to wear the yoke no longer. The British Parliament and King had as zealous partisans and friends among us, as they had at home. It became necessary, in some way, to ascertain who were the friends of our own, and the mother country. The Pledge was suggested; and, acting on a test of divine origin, they who refused to sign it were set down as opposed to their country and the maintenance of her rights. If ever there was a "time that tried mens' souls," it was when they grasped the "gray-goose quill" to sign their death warrant if they failed, or their liberty if successful. At that period, even the most violent patriot must have looked upon the undertaking as desperate and almost hopeless, with but one chance out of ten in his favor. But they were men of a bygone and an iron age, upon whom the world would not look again. They had made up their minds to die rather than submit; and when men of such indomitable energy of mind once deliberately resolve, their destiny is fixed" (100-101).

Fully one-third of those eligible in Dutchess County (which included what is now Putnam County) to proclaim their loyalty instead took the side of the British. The owners of Lot No. 5 of the Philipse Patent, including what is now Mt. Nimham (Mary Philipse Morris, and her husband, Col. Roger

Morris) were prominent loyalists during the Revolution, supporting the British Crown. So the patriots of Mt. Nimham (including James Russell, John Russell, Lt. Thomas Russell, Robert Russell, James Smalley, his sons James Jr., Isaiah, and Zachariah, Abraham Smalley, Samuel Hawkins, General James Townsend, Captain Elijah Townsend, Captain Solomon Hopkins, Reuben Hopkins, Jonathan Hopkins Sr., Jonathan Hopkins Jr., Joseph Hopkins, Jeremiah Hopkins, Captain Elisha Cole Jr., Elisha Cole III, Reuben Cole, Ebenezer Cole, Joseph Cole, Daniel Cole, Jacob Van Scoy, and Ebenezer Brown), all tenant farmers working on the Upper Highlands Patent (Lot No. 5), had to make a life and death decision for themselves and their families.

These patriots decided to cast their lot with the patriotic cause, with most of them serving in Colonel Henry Ludington's 7th Regiment of the Dutchess County Militia. They served in defense of the Highlands, in the protection of Peekskill and Fishkill, and were also responsible for preventing British agents from infiltrating the Highlands through the numerous mountain passes, including Whang Hollow, Peekskill Hollow, and Wiccopee Pass. They trained on the first Monday of each month for four hours in the flatland area near Ludington's mill, known as the parade ground, which is now the intersection of Routes 52 and 84. There was also a parade ground southwest of Mt. Nimham, on the old Boyd farm where Boyd's Reservoir stands today on Route 301. This was also very near the location of the early Native settlement where Chief Nimham was believed to have lived for a period of time between the 1750s and 1770s.

The militia was active in the policing of the Highlands, to prevent British incursions and Tory acts of sabotage, and to deal with the "Cowboys" and "Skinners," roving bands of miscreants who stole from the farmers and terrorized the countryside. The "Cowboys" generally sided with the loyalists, while the "Skinners" were usually associated with the patriots. However, these looters were mostly taking advantage of the chaotic times for their own gain. The "Skinners" were so named because of their penchant to steal clothing from their victims (which was in short supply), while the "Cowboys" were more likely to steal cattle to provision the British troops.

The patriots of Mt. Nimham also utilized the mountaintop to communicate with their fellow patriots across the lower Hudson Valley through the use of fires that served as beacons to send signals and sound alarms through the network of neighboring hilltops.

According to Pelletreau's description of the Hopkins homestead:

"South of Cole's Mills, on the road to Carmel, is the old homestead farm, which originally belonged to the Hopkins family. It was here that Captain Solomon Hopkins lived during the Revolution. He was the brother-in-law of Enoch Crosby, the hero of Cooper's "The Spy," and after the war he purchased 341 acres of land in the Morris Lot No. 5 from the Commissioners of Forfeiture. The homestead descended from Solomon Hopkins (who died September 22d, 1792, aged 52) to his son, Jeremiah, who in turn left it to his son, Abraham, who sold it to his brother, Solomon, and it came to his son, Addison J., who sold it in 1859 to Polly D. Haight, wife of Joseph Haight, to whom it now belongs. It was in the old house which stood on the site of the present residence of Mr. Haight that the murderous attack was made upon Enoch Crosby, which came near ending his days. The old house was torn down and the present residence built about 1874" (677).

The Solomon Hopkins farm was located on the Philipstown Turnpike, on what is now Route 301, across from the West Branch Reservoir (see Illustration 4). It consisted of a combination house and inn, which was the scene of several encounters between the patriots and the loyalist Cowboys. It was reported that Hopkins would leave the upper window of his home open to allow his brother-in-law, Enoch Crosby, also known as Cooper's "Harvey Birch" (The Spy), to enter as he pleased, unobserved.

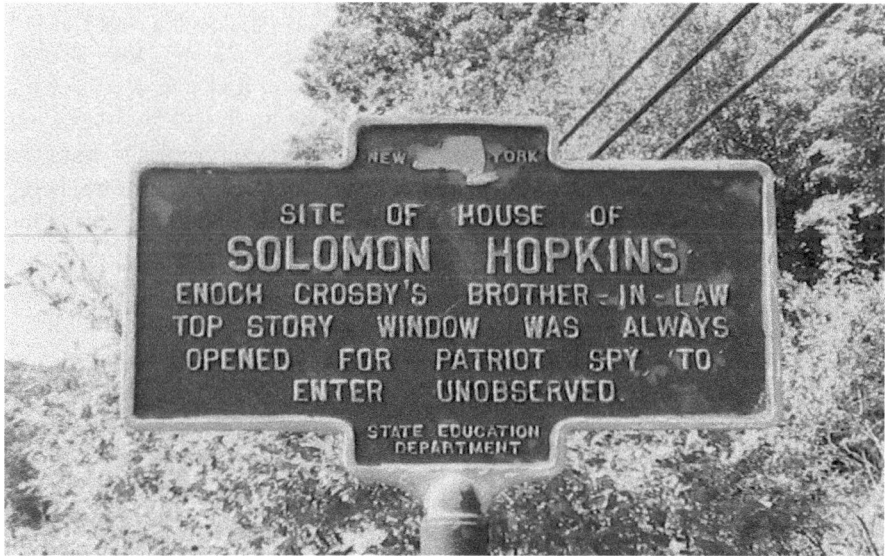

Illustration 4: New York State Historical Marker for the Captain Solomon Hopkins House Site on Route 301 in Kent (*Photo by author*)

Solomon Hopkins served with distinction during the War of Independence, initially as a Quartermaster with the 6th Regiment under Morris Graham and

Colonel Roswell Hopkins, then later with Colonel Ludington's 7th Regiment in 1778 as a First Lieutenant, and then once again with the 6th Regiment. He was a lineal descendant of Stephen Hopkins, one of the Mayflower Pilgrims (Town of Kent Bicentennial Committee, 67).

1776: On March 12th, Elijah Townsend was appointed First Lieutenant of "Beat Number 4," under Captain John Crane, of the 7th Regiment of the Dutchess County Militia, headed by Colonel Henry Ludington (Pelletreau, 698). He would eventually rise to the rank of Adjutant under Col. Ludington's command, and would serve as the patriarch of the Townsend family on Mt. Nimham (Roberts, 150).

On August 8th, the New York Colonial Legislature issued a war measure directing the militias to secure the mountain passes in the Highlands. Following the British troop movements north of New York City, on October 10th, it was further ordered that regiments *"hold one-half of their several Regiments in Readiness to march at an hour's notice with five days provisions"* (Johnson, 80). Thus, on October 20th, Colonel Ludington's regiment, including the patriots from Mt. Nimham, moved from the Highlands to Peekskill, and then on to the Kingsbridge area. They then moved northward to engage the British in the Battle of Chatterton Hill in White Plains, known today as the Battle of White Plains, on October 28th. Col. Ludington himself served as one of General Washington's aides in this conflict. When Washington's army was turned back by the British, Washington moved his men across the Hudson River and into New Jersey, drawing the British toward him to avoid allowing them to follow the patriots northward into the Highlands. Ludington's regiment then returned home to the Highlands to deal with the Tories who were described as being "ominously strong" with the British victories in and around New York City. Even though the British took Washington's bait, they still devised a plan to march up the eastern side of the Hudson, avoiding the patriots' strong points of defense at West Point. So the Mt. Nimham patriots under Ludington's command stayed at North Castle until word of the British rout at Trenton was received (Johnson, 76-85).

During the White Plains campaign, "The Spy" Enoch Crosby was first enlisted to serve his country as a member of the secret service. After learning of a Tory plot to raise a British Army unit in Westchester County, Crosby pretended to be a captive of Captain Micah Townsend. Crosby was allowed to "escape" and return to the Tory camp as a "proven Loyalist" in order to learn more details of their plot. Crosby then relayed the details to Townsend, who then took them all prisoner before the plot could be fully hatched. The prisoners were then marched to Fishkill, with Crosby continuing to pretend to be a Loyalist. The prisoners were brought before John Jay, who chaired a special committee for detecting conspiracies. Crosby was eventually bailed out by Jonathan Hopkins, the uncle of Crosby's brother-in-law, Captain Solomon Hopkins (Johnson, 120-122). This allowed him to maintain his "loyalist cover" for future missions in defense of his country. He then worked with John Russell to infiltrate the command of Beverly Robinson, the scoundrel Loyalist who had helped his Philipse in-laws to secure their theft of the Nochpeem ancestral homeland on and around Mt. Nimham. However, this "John Russell" was not the same individual who lived on the southern end of Mt. Nimham with his brothers, the patriots Thomas, Robert, and James Russell.

1777: Having spent much of the previous fall on duty protecting the Highlands, on January 3rd the patriots from Mt. Nimham were ordered *"to employ such detachments of the militia of Dutchess County as are not in actual service . . . for inquiring into, detecting and defeating all conspiracies which may be found against the liberties of America"* (Johnson, 86).

On Friday April 25th, a force of 2,000 British troops landed at Compo, near Fairfield, Connecticut, under the command of General Tryon, the former British Governor of New York, under whom Ludington had once held a commission. They marched hastily inland, and on the afternoon of April 26th they reached Danbury. Danbury was being used as a storage depot by the Continental Army. Supplies such as clothing, medicine, tents and ammunition, as well as pork, flour, and molasses, were kept there. On the night of Saturday, April 26, 1777, the redcoats started to attack. Only 150 colonial soldiers were there to defend the town. The redcoats, in one of their less valiant and sober moments, began burning the private residences in the city in an unrestrained orgy, fueled in part by the looted spirits they had consumed in large quantities. Loyalist homes were spared by the marking of a red "X" on their front doors. Reinforcements were desperately needed.

A messenger brought the news of the sacking of Danbury to Colonel Ludington around 8pm on the evening of the 26th. He had to summon his volunteers, who were back on their farms performing their spring plantings, but he himself was needed to prepare for the twenty-five mile march and to be present as the militia assembled. So, according to Ludington family members (as later reported by Willis Fletcher Johnson in his 1907 memoir of Colonel Ludington), 16 year-old Sybil Ludington, Colonel Ludington's daughter, took her horse on a 42-plus mile ride through Frederickstown (Kent and Carmel), including Horsepound Road (the main north-south route), to summon the militia in response to the British burning of Danbury and its surrounding towns. She made sure to reach the homes of the militia's officers, who then helped to spread the alert to the rest of the patriots. She faced tremendous danger from Cowboys and Skinners, and from Hessian troops who had deserted from the British ranks. As she saw campfires along the way, she had to detour through the woods in the thick of the night, in a cold April rain, changing horses along the way.

Word quickly spread to the families along what we now call Coles Mills and Gipsy Trail Roads. By daybreak the next day, the enraged patriots of Mt. Nimham joined approximately 400 of their fellow comrades, marching from Ludington's Mill to Danbury via Mooney Hill Road to what is now Route 311, down Route 22 in Patterson to Doansburgh Road and Sherwood Road into Connecticut. The next morning they encountered the British at Ridgefield. They were short of ammunition and were outnumbered by the British three to one. But they practiced the same tactics that Paul Revere's levies at Concord and Lexington found so effective. Their scattered sharpshooter fire from behind trees, fences and stone walls, harassed the British sorely, and made their retreat to their ships at Long Island Sound resemble a rout. General Benedict Arnold had his horse shot from under him during the battle. General Wooster suffered a wound which took his life several days later. An American boy was captured and later escaped to tell of 500 casualties among the enemy, as he saw them carried on board the fleet.

As noted by Alexander Hamilton, the aide decamps to General Washington, in a letter written to New York Governor Morris: *"I congratulate you on the Danbury expedition. The stores destroyed there have been purchased at a pretty high price to the enemy . . . The people of New York considered the affair in the light of a defeat to the British troops"* (Johnson, 89-91).

In June, there were renewed indications that the British were planning another attempt to gain control of the Hudson River. The Mt. Nimham patriots were ordered to Peekskill to strengthen the defenses in the Highlands. But this was a critical time for the farmers' corn crop, and their appeals were heeded as they were excused from this call-up. But by early October, Ludington's regiment found themselves defending Wrights Mills, located between White Plains and Tarrytown. With about 233 men in attendance with him, he faced a British incursion in Tarrytown led once again by General Tryon and 3,000 British troops. Tryon sent a message to Ludington, offering his men mercy if they were to surrender. Ludington replied that *"as long as we had a man alive I was determined to oppose them and they might come on as soon as they pleased"* (Johnson, 103).

The British then used fog to their advantage to transfer their troops to the western side of the river, assaulting the patriot positions at Fort Clinton and

Fort Montgomery. This British victory was considered the most impressive of their campaigns throughout the war. General Putnam escaped into the mountains, and General Clinton narrowly avoided capture. British General Clinton, after ordering the burning of Kingston, however, failed to take full advantage of this victory, and instead returned to New York City. This fateful error left British General Burgoyne stranded up the river as he fought against the patriot forces led by Generals Gates, Arnold, Schuyler and Morgan.

On October 13th, British General Burgoyne formally surrendered his army at Saratoga. This represented a major turning point in the war, and from this time forward the patriots controlled the all important North River, now known as the Hudson River.

1778: On May 1st, Colonel Ludington sent a letter to Governor Clinton requesting that Elijah Townsend be formally commissioned as a Captain in his regiment. Gov. Clinton promptly replied his approval of Townsend's commission (Johnson, 160-161).

Meanwhile, General George Washington had formed a light infantry company made up of militiamen and a few hundred Native Americans, designed to strike at the enemy quickly and with devastating results. This concept was based upon the strategy employed by Rogers' Rangers during the Seven Years War, which had originally included Chief Daniel Nimham and his Wappinger brothers. In the late summer of 1778, Washington gathered his army at White Plains to prevent the British from moving northward out of New York City. The battle to control the Hudson River, then known as the North River, would be the centerpiece of the strategy adopted by both sides in the war. If the British controlled the river, they could split the colonies in two and conquer the divided and weakened patriots. Chief Daniel Nimham, along with his son Abraham and his band of Wappinger brothers, had been harassing the British as they moved northward.

As Pelletreau described the momentous events that would follow:

"It was on the 30th of August, 1778, that Nimham and his warrior band went forth to the field of their last battle. On that day they met with a scouting party of British under Colonel Emerick, and after a fierce engagement compelled them to retreat. On the following morning the whole of the British force at Kings Bridge was ordered out and the larger part was placed in an ambuscade, while Emerick was sent forward to decoy his assailants of the previous day. In the extreme northern part of the annexed

portion of the city of New York, is a high elevation of land known as Cortlandt's Ridge. Winding through the valleys and emptying into the Harlem River, near Kings Bridge, is a stream that has borne from earliest times the name of Tippets Brook. The wooded heights and the banks of the stream were the scenes of a most sanguinary conflict. The attempt to draw the Indians into the ambuscade failed, and upon their advance the British troops had scarcely time to fall into rank. The Indians lined the fences and commenced firing upon the forces under Colonel Emerick. The Queen's Rangers moved rapidly to gain the heights, and Tarleton advanced with the Hussars and his famous Legion of Cavalry. This being reported to Lieutenant Colonel Simcoe, he directed Major Ross to conduct his corps on the heights, and advancing to the road arrived within ten yards of Nimham and his men. Up to this time they had been intent on the attack by Colonel Emerick. They now gave a yell and fired upon the advancing enemy and wounded five, including Colonel Simcoe.

They were driven from the fence, and Tarleton rushed upon them with his cavalry and pursued them down Cortlandt's Ridge. Here Tarleton himself had a narrow escape. Striking at one of the fugitives, he lost his balance and fell from his horse. Fortunately for him the Indian had no bayonet and his musket was discharged. A captain of a company of American soldiers was taken prisoner with some of his men, and a company under Major Stewart, who afterwards distinguished himself at the storming of Stony Point, left the Indians and fled. The engagement was renewed with the fiercest vigor. The cavalry charged the ridge with overwhelming numbers, but were bravely resisted. As the cavalry rode them down, the Indians seized their foes, dragged them from their horses, to join them in death. In a swamp, not far from the brook, Nimham made his last stand. When he saw the Grenadiers closing upon him and all hope of successful resistance gone, he called out to his people to flee, but as for himself, 'I am an aged tree, I will die here.' Being attacked by Simcoe he wounded that officer, but was shot and killed by Wright, his orderly Hussar. In this fearful fray the power of the tribe was forever broken. More than forty of the Indians were killed or desperately wounded in the fight, and when the next morning dawned, there, still and cold in death, on the field he had defended so bravely, lay the last sachem of the Wappingers.

The place where they crossed Tippets Brook is still known as Indian Bridge, and an opening in the Cortlandt woods yet bears the name of Indian Field, and there the dead were buried. It is said that the spirit of the sachem still haunts the field of his last battle, and that the sound of his war cry still rises on the midnight air, and greets the ear of the belated traveler as he treads on his lonely way" (85-86).

A few days later, the dogs of the farm's owner, by the name of Daniel

DeVoe, came home with blood in their mouths and carrying assorted body parts. In fact, the bodies of Nimham, his son Abraham, and the other Native American Indian heroes had been left to rot on the battlefield. Some accounts claim the deceased Native patriots totaled nearly 40 men. A descendant of the original farmer, historian Thomas DeVoe, wrote in an 1880 article:

"The greatest struggle, was on the second field north of Daniel DeVoe's house, where the bodies of some seventeen Indians lay, cut and hacked to death; besides many others, who were killed and wounded in their attempt to escape in several directions. It was a terrible conflict, or rather a slaughter of about thirty Indians...Many years afterwards, this fight was a frequent subject of conversation by those of the families who had visited the fields immediately after the conflict..."

The bodies of the slain Indian patriots were taken to a portion of the field, interred with stones placed on top, *"not as a monument, but to protect the bodies from further desecration"* (DeVoe, 194)." The DeVoe family used such a cairn as was their Scottish tradition. Today, a stone monument erected by the Daughters of the American Revolution marks this location in what is now the northeast corner of Van Cortlandt Park (Tarbox, 5-6).

As Pelletreau, writing in the year 1886, concluded his moving tribute:

"A person who stands on the high land in Carmel, south of Lake Gleneida, sees far to the northwest, three lofty mountains that tower above all the country round. To the middle peak, which is the highest, we have given the name of the last Sachem of the tribe that once ruled all the lands that can be seen from its highest summit: and we trust that in honor of his valor, and of the faith sealed with his blood, on the field where he fought for the liberty of America, it will bear to all future time the name of Mount Nimham" (86).

1779: In June, following the British capture of Verplanck's Point, the Mt. Nimham militiamen were called up to fortify the Crompond area. Before daylight on June 24, they were surprised by a contingent of 200 British Cavalry, who had advanced from New York City. Nearly 30 militiamen were killed or wounded in the sharp skirmish. Another 130 British light infantry supported the cavalry. Another attack followed while the patriots were having breakfast at a nearby church which was being used as an arsenal. After these encounters, the regiment marched back home. Once there, they became even more engaged in the "cold war" between the Tory spies, their sympathizers, and the patriots.

Loyalist raids continued in the Highlands, as the British Army quartered in

New York City needed to be provisioned. The patriots' resentment over having their livestock and crops stolen from them soon began to boil over. And so, following the decisive Battle of Saratoga in the fall of 1777, on October 22, 1779, the New York Colonial Legislature passed an "Act of Attainder", confiscating the property of the most prominent of the royalists, including Colonel Roger and Mary Philipse Morris, and Beverly and Susannah Philipse Robinson, banishing them from the State. Mary Philipse Morris and her husband owned Lot No. 5 of the Upper Highland Patent of the Philipse Patent, which included Mt. Nimham. By the provisions of this act, John Hathorn, Samuel Dodge and Daniel Graham were appointed commissioners to sell the confiscated and forfeited estates. They became known as the "Commissioners of Forfeiture." In most cases, the lands were sold to the parties (tenants of the Philipses) who were already in possession of the various farms. The displaced Philipse family at first settled in New York City, then fled to England following the final British surrender at Yorktown (Pelletreau, 92).

1780: In May of 1780, Colonel Ludington's regiment was again activated to protect West Point. After assembling at Fishkill, the Mt. Nimham patriots made their way to West Point and served there for approximately two weeks.

In implementing the Act of Attainder, the Commissioners of Forfeiture sold the land previously leased to the tenant farmers of the Philipse/Morris family. In addition, some veterans of the Revolution were given a land grant of 80 acres, in lieu of pay for their services. It is reported that the sale price established by the Commissioners of Forfeiture was set at $1.00 per acre. Even though the tenants felt the price was too high, their intense desire to own their farms helped them to overcome their trepidation. The patriots James Smalley, James Townsend, and Lt. Thomas Russell, all tenant farmers on Lot No. 5 of the Upper Highlands Patent of the Philipse Patent, purchased 232, 352, and 166 acres, respectively, on the high ridge now known as Mt. Nimham between 1782 and the end of 1783 (Pelletreau, 95-96) (see Illustration 5). James Smalley owned the western and top portions of the mountain, including the location where the fire tower stands today. His property extended southward to just beyond the West Branch of the Croton River. James Townsend owned a portion of the top to the north of the Smalley property, including the area known as "Big Hill," in addition to the northwest side of the mountain. Meanwhile, the Russells owned most of the property along Coles Mills Road, to the south and east of the Smalleys.

The patriot Samuel Hawkins purchased a 100-acre site at the northern end of the mountain along what is now called Maynard Road, in addition to another 54-acre parcel just a bit to the east in Whang Hollow. Just south of the Russells was the farm of the patriot Jacob VanScoy, who purchased 88 acres from the Commissioners of Forfeiture. And to the east of VanScoy, near Smokey Hollow, was the property of the patriot Captain Solomon Hopkins.

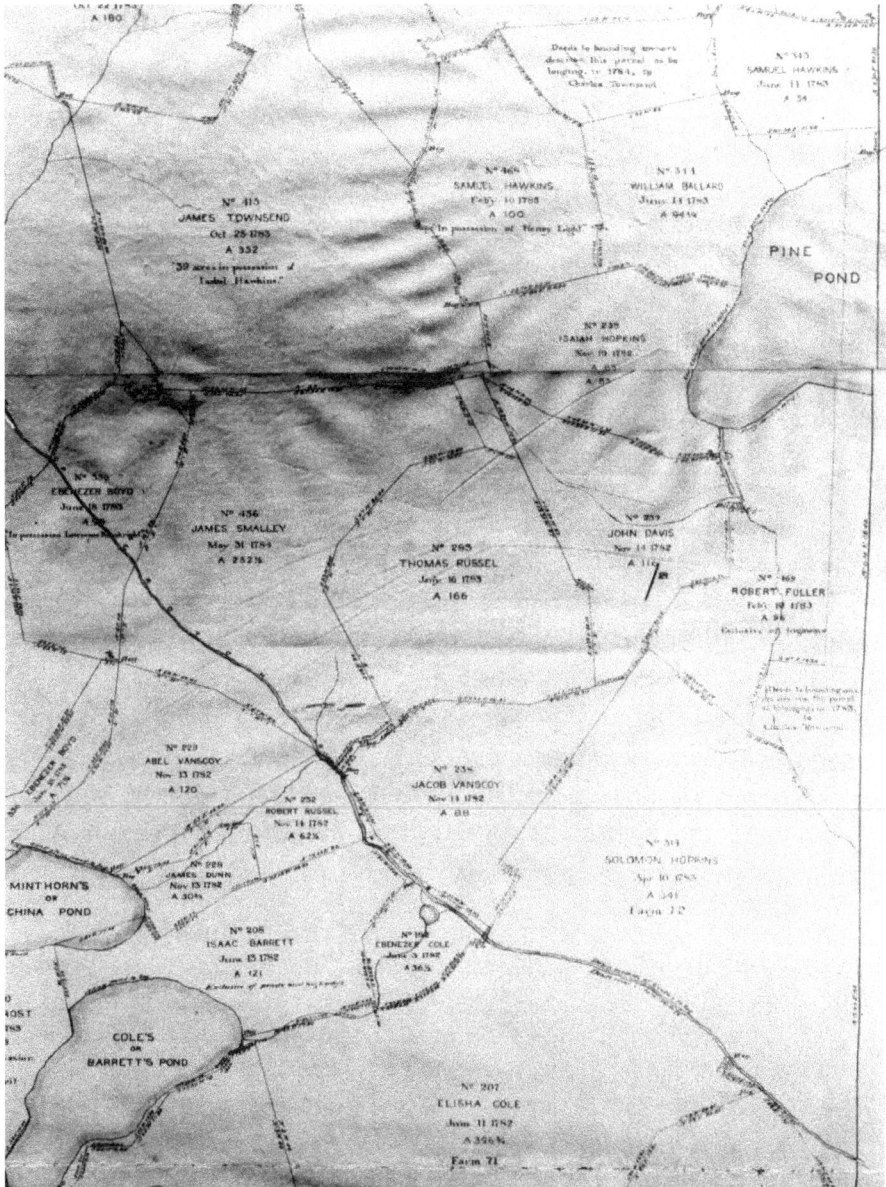

Illustration 5: Excerpt from the Commissioners of Forfeiture Map (as reconstructed in 1887 by Henry Conklin, from the original Forfeiture Deeds) (*Courtesy of the Putnam County Historian's Office*)

Their neighbors to the east, and just west of Pine Pond, were the patriot Isaiah Hopkins (83 acres), William Ballard (94 ¾ acres), and the patriot John Davis (116 acres). Just south of Pine Pond were the farms of the patriot Robert Fuller (96 acres), Aaron Brown (64 acres), his father, the patriot Ebenezer Brown (63 ½ acres), and Aaron's brother, Daniel (50 ¼ acres). To the northwest was the farm of Joseph Farrington (160 acres), who also owned the early mills that would eventually form the epicenter of the Farmers Mills community. Also located to the north was the 180-acre farm of the patriot Captain Consider Cushman and his wife, Phebe Townsend Cushman, the daughter of Uriah Townsend. Uriah Townsend was the patriarch of the Townsend clan that owned a string of farms along what became known as "Townsend Ridge", which forms the north-eastern wall of Whang Hollow, where the "Rockridge Farm" and the "Winter Garden Farm" are located today.

The patriot Cole family owned several farms and mills on the southern end of the mountain, along the West Branch of the Croton River. The patriot Ebenezer Cole owned 36 ½ acres, including the mills and the millpond which constituted "Coles Mills". The patriot Rev. Elisha Cole Jr. owned two lots totaling 514 ¼ acres adjacent to his son's property. His other sons, the patriots Daniel and Joseph, owned a 230-acre lot directly south of their father's property.

Finally, to the west of the Smalley and Townsend farms was the property of the patriot Ebenezer Boyd, who owned several lots along the West Branch of the Croton River.

However, property boundaries frequently changed over the years due to deaths, marriages and other subdivisions of the land. For the period between the late 1700s up to the late 1800s, the mountain would be known as "Smalley Hill."

Unfortunately, the Native American Indian veterans of the war were not entitled to the same land grants as were the European veterans. With the death of the patriot Chief Daniel Nimham and his fellow warriors in August of 1778, the Wappingers' pursuit to regain part of their ancestral homeland lost to the Philipse family was dealt the final death blow. Daniel's younger brother, Aaron, became the leader of the remaining Wappinger following the death of his brother. He married a woman from the Oneida nation, and hence the name "Nimham" eventually became known as "Ninham" in the Oneida tradition.

In yet another case of tragic irony, these two tribes, the only ones that actively supported the American cause in the War of Independence, were among the first of the Eastern tribes to be forced westward during the government's removal policy in the early 1800s (Grumet, 91).

Half of the Mahican and Wappinger men of military age were killed fighting for the American cause in the War of Independence. The new nation's gratitude for their sacrifice was brief. They were not allowed to become citizens after the war. By 1786 the last groups of the Stockbridge and Wappinger had been forced to leave Massachusetts and resettle with the Oneida in upstate New York, near Utica. But they were eventually driven from that location by the local colonists. A small band of Wappinger would remain in the Mt. Nimham area, eventually living in a settlement west of Farmers Mills, near Sagamore Lake, until about 1812. This settlement was located south of the Philipstown Turnpike, now Route 301, near the current Kent-Putnam Valley border.

During the years which followed, the Oneida and Stockbridge slowly lost their lands to speculators and the State of New York. In 1822 they relocated to a reservation established for the Oneida near Green Bay, Wisconsin. In 1856 a separate reservation was created for the Munsee on lands purchased from the Menominee by the United States (Sultzman).

The incredibly inspiring, and tragically ironic story of Daniel Nimham's life and supreme sacrifice must never be forgotten. Instead of advocating violence against the settlers and the aristocratic patent holders who had seized his ancestral homeland, he pursued justice for his people through the very institutions that denied his rights as a human being. First through the colonial court, then across the ocean to the King's Court in London, and back again in the colonial courts, justice was always denied. Like his Biblical namesake, he was a man caught between two worlds. He always pursued peaceful means of settling the land disputes between the Wappinger and the elitist patent holders, but he also fought with bravery and determination in pursuit of freedom and our independence. In the end, this amazing man and his brethren helped to gain independence and land-owning rights for the very settlers who would take possession of the Nochpeem ancestral homeland. Theirs is truly an inspiring story which must live forever in American history, and most especially in the history of the town of Kent and the lower Hudson Valley. We honor the supreme sacrifice they made for our independence. They are true, unsung patriots, who must never be forgotten.

1781: On May 1st of this year, Colonel Ludington wrote to Governor Clinton, complaining of large parties of "robbers," who had been attacking farms in the nearby mountains for the previous four weeks. This forced him to call out the regiment to counter these attacks. In describing the plight of his men and their families, *"at best the Regiment are very poor when compared with other Regiments and are called on to raise an equal number with the others, when I can affirm that ten members of Col. Brinckerhoff's Regiment is able to purchase the whole of mine. In this unequal way, I have been obliged to turn out my men until they are so much impoverished that they almost despair. It seems the power of Earth and Hell was let loose against me and my Regiment"* (Johnson, 178).

But on October 19, 1781, their despair was finally relieved when British General Cornwallis surrendered his force of 7,000 men to the patriots in Yorktown, Virginia. The War of Independence formally ended on September 3, 1783, with the signing of the Treaty of Paris. The last British troops left New York City on November 25, 1783.

1782: The Kent & Fishkill Baptist Church was formed in the area then known as "Milltown," and later known as "Farmers Mills." Originally called "The Baptist Church of Christ in Kent and Fishkill," the first church building was erected in 1800, and was later replaced in 1840. The first pastor was Elder John Lawrence. Many residents of the Mt. Nimham area would worship here over the years, and some former residents are buried in the church cemetery (Pelletreau, 684).

1790: The Federal Census of 1790 listed the following families on and around Mt. Nimham:

Head of Household Last Name	First Name	Males Over 16	Males Under 16	Females
Brown	Ebenezer	4	2	4
Cole	Reuben	1	2	3
Cole	Nathan	1	4	5
Cole	Joshua	1	1	2
Cole	Daniel	2	3	7
Cole	John	2	2	2
Cole	Elisha	4	4	4
Cole	Joseph	2	4	4
Ferris	Reuben	3	1	4
Hawkins	Samuel	1	1	3
Hopkins	Isaiah	2	0	2

Head of Household		Males Over 16	Males Under 16	Females
Last Name	First Name			
Russell	James	1	0	2
Russell	Abijah	1	0	2
Russell	James Jr.	2	2	6
Russell	Thomas	2	2	5
Smalley	Isaiah	1	1	2
Smalley	James	1	0	3
Smalley	James Jr.	1	3	2
Smalley	Zachariah	1	0	2
Townsend	James	3	1	6
Townsend	Elijah	1	4	4

1792: The patriot Captain Solomon Hopkins, who owned a 341-acre farm on what is now Route 301 just east of the Coles Mills area, extending northward up the southern slope of the mountain, passed away on September 29th at the age of 53. Captain Hopkins was the brother-in-law of "The Spy" Enoch Crosby. It is reported that Enoch would frequently stay at the Hopkins house and inn during his days of intrigue throughout the Revolution. One night, he and Hopkins were nearly beaten to death by a group of Tory Cowboys who had come to kill him and Hopkins. Luckily, both survived, and the assailants were dispatched by Hopkins' neighbors along the bank of the Croton River (Barnum). Captain Hopkins is buried in the Gilead Burial Ground in Carmel along with his wife, near Enoch Crosby's plot.

1793: On June 7th, the Mt. Nimham patriot Lt. Col. Elijah Townsend was named the commanding officer of the 7th Regiment of the Dutchess County Militia (Johnson, 204). Henry Ludington Jr. served as his lieutenant.

1798: The patriot Reuben Hopkins passed away on July 2nd at the age of 30. It is reported that he accidentally drowned in a tanning vat. He was the son of the patriot Captain Solomon Hopkins and Elizabeth Crosby Hopkins. His uncle was "The Spy" Enoch Crosby, who had many adventures on the Hopkins farm, located near Coles Mills at the southern end of Mt. Nimham. Reuben is buried in the Gilead Burying Ground.

The patriot Captain Consider Cushman, the owner of a 180-acre farm just north of Mt. Nimham, served as Supervisor of Frederick (Kent) from 1798 to 1802.

Chapter 4

A Summary of the Farms and Farm Life in the Mount Nimham Area

Following the dislocation of the local Nochpeem population, the farms of the Smalley, Townsend, Hawkins, Light, Russell, Brown, Hopkins, Bailey, Cargin, Wixon, Northrup and Cole families dominated the Mt. Nimham area for most of the period from the 1760s until the early 1900s. Other families, such as Ferris, Tompkins, Dean, Cargain and McDaniels, were also found on and around the mountain at various times. The mountain was ringed by cow-paths and cart-paths now known as Mt. Nimham Court, Coles Mills Road (reported to have originally been a Native trail), Smalley Corners Road, Maynard Road, Cole Shears Road and Clear Pool Road. Some of these are still in existence, while others are no more than trails in the woods today.

In the early days, the road that we now know as "Mt. Nimham Court" was actually part of one continuous road that stretched from Gipsy Trail Road down to the Philipstown Turnpike (what is now Route 301), known as "the road to Coles Mills." In the 1925 New York State Census, it was listed as "Coles Mills Hill Road," and today it is known as "Coles Mills Road." The road leading to the top of the mountain was just a cart path until the CCC and New York State expanded it in order to build the fire tower in 1940.

Over the years, the neighboring families on Mt. Nimham and the surrounding area intermarried with each other, so they nearly all became members of the same extended family within just a few generations.

The Smalley family dominated the top and western areas of the mountain throughout the late 1700s and 1800s. The patriarch of the family was the patriot James Smalley, and his patriot sons, James Jr., Isaiah, and Zachariah. They founded a burgeoning Smalley clan that would serve in every capacity of civic life in the town of Kent. Their names are found on every historical map surrounding Mt. Nimham throughout the 1800s. Their descendants would serve our country in both the Mexican War and Civil War. The dominating presence and patriotism of this clan led to the naming of the mountain as "Smalley Hill" throughout this period. The corbelled stone chamber found along the road leading to the top of the mountain was most likely constructed by the Smalleys, although it was also used at various times by the Townsends, Browns and Deans. The Smalley family name continues to be remembered in this area through "Smalley Corners Road," the "Smalley Burial Ground," and the "Smalley Inn" in the Hamlet of Carmel.

Gen. James Townsend and his brother, Lt. Col. Elijah Townsend, were the patriarchs of the Townsend family on Mt. Nimham. James Townsend, who was married to Priscilla Ann Cole, the daughter of the patriot Rev. Elisha Cole Jr., was mostly interested in the mountain for its mining prospects. Their original property on the mountain covered the north-northwestern area of the mountain, including much of "Big Hill." However, the Townsend family would eventually own the "Fairview Farm" on the corner of what is now called Mt. Nimham Court and Coles Mills Road, where the NYS DEC parking lot is located today, although it is believed that this site may have originally been owned by the Russell family. The patriot Lt. Thomas Russell's granddaughter, Ada, married Lt. Col. Elijah Townsend's son, Joshua, possibly introducing the Townsends to this property. The stone structure located adjacent to the parking area is not a corbelled stone chamber – instead, it is an explosives bunker, originally intended to store munitions used for mining activities conducted by the Townsend family on the mountain during the late 1800s and early 1900s. It was also used as a smokehouse by the tenants of the Townsends in the early 1900s.

The Townsends were stalwarts of the Democratic Party, and served in many civic positions over the years. James Townsend was best known for his mining activities on Mt. Nimham and at Tilly Foster in Southeast. The mountain still shows the evidence of this mining activity, especially along the steep rocky ridge lines on the northwestern and northeastern portions of the mountain. According to Pelletreau, *"Near the north end of the reservoir, upon a road now obliterated, stood, in the beginning of this century, a forge and small furnace for melting iron. This was owned by James Townsend, and he was the first man who used ore from the Tilly Foster Mine. Relics of the old forge may yet be seen at low water"* (682).

Throughout most of the 1800s, Stephen Townsend (1810-1893, the son of Joshua and the grandson of the patriot Lt. Col. Elijah Townsend) was a fixture at what is now the intersection of Mt. Nimham Court and Coles Mills Road, and his name is listed on the various historical maps of Kent published in the 1800s. He was married to Mary (Polly) Smalley, the daughter of Isaac and Elizabeth Russell Smalley (and the granddaughter of the patriot Zachariah Smalley). Their descendents, including son Coleman ("Judge Townsend") and grandson Hamilton Fish Townsend, carried on the tradition on the old family homestead into the early 1900s. The old Townsend farm has left remnants which exist to this day. According to the late Ken Townsend, the grandson of Judge Townsend, their family farm was known as the "Fairview Farm" (Katherine Kane, interview with Ken and Ella Townsend). The Townsend family of the 1900s continued to serve in a variety of civic positions. Ken served as the Highway Supervisor of Kent for many years, while his brother, Clarence James Townsend, served as Town Historian, in the mid to late 1900s.

John Wixon, and later his son, Wright Wixon, owned a farm on what is now the end of Cole Shears Court on the western edge of the mountain. They were descendants of Peleg Wixon of Carmel. A stone chamber which faces out toward the road, directly adjacent to the road itself, bears witness to the existence of this farm.

The patriot Samuel Hawkins, and later his nephews (Henry E., Moseman, and his twin, "Night" Light), owned property at the northern end of the mountain, along what is known today as Maynard Road. The Light brothers were raised by their father's sister, Abigail, and her husband, Samuel Hawkins. Henry Light later owned the 100-acre farm previously owned by his Uncle Samuel, and the map of 1854 shows a "milk house" at that location. Remnants of his farm can still be seen today in the form of a corbelled stone chamber, a stone-fenced corral or barn foundation, and an old well. Moseman Light owned the farm that was located at the current Gipsy Trail Club administration building site near the corner of Maynard Road and Gipsy Trail Road. This may also have been a portion of the original Samuel Hawkins farm. This site would later be owned by Isaac Smalley, Jr.

Both of these Light brothers married into the Ferris family. The Ferris farm was located along Gipsy Trail Road on the eastern side of the mountain, where the "Pine View Farm" is located today. This property was previously owned by James D. Hyatt. Henry Light married Susan Jane Ferris, and Moseman married her sister, Sarah Maria Ferris. They were the daughters of John and Phoebe Lee Ferris. It is believed that they had a brother, Darius Alonzo Ferris, who married Malinda Light, the sister of Henry, Moseman and Night. Darius Ferris was a fixture on the eastern side of Mt. Nimham throughout the mid to late 1800s. It is believed that the Ferris' lineage included the patriots Ezra Ferris and his father, Colonel Reuben Ferris.

"Night" Light, the great-grandfather of Bettymarie Light Behr, married Sarah Jane Smalley, the daughter of Isaac and Elizabeth Brown Smalley. Their farm was located along Whang Hollow Road.

On the lower eastern base of Mt. Nimham, the Brown family owned three farms: just south of Pine Pond were the farms of Aaron Brown (64 acres), his father, the patriot Ebenezer Brown (63 ½ acres), and Aaron's brother, Daniel (50 ¼ acres). Another brother, Stephen Brown, owned property further up the eastern side of the mountain, near the corbelled stone chamber, just above the Stephen Townsend farm site. The mine located south of Mt.

Nimham Court was dubbed "Brown's Quarry" on the maps of the 1800s. The mine just north of Mt. Nimham Court was known as "Brown's Silver Mine Hole."

The Russells owned a farm which encompassed most of Coles Mills Road. Over time, the epicenter of their farm became located about three-quarters of a mile down the old road from the DEC parking area. This farm was originally owned by the patriot Lt. Thomas Russell, the uncle of Morris. This farm was in close proximity to the farms of his brothers, the patriots James and John Russell. In addition, Morris Russell, the son of the patriot James Russell and his wife, Elizabeth Light Russell, can be found there on the maps of 1854 and 1867. Morris was married to Mahala Brown, the granddaughter of the patriot Ebenezer Brown from Gipsy Trail Road. There still exists a partially standing stone structure directly on the road at the old farm site, the stone walkway leading to the old house, and a partially collapsed corbelled stone chamber further north up the road.

Just south of the Russell farm, near what is now the intersection of Coles Mills Road and Route 301, stood the Cole farm and Coles Mills on the West Branch of the Croton River. As previously noted, Rev. Elisha Cole Jr. came from Cape Cod in 1747, settling at the southern base of Mt. Nimham, and built a mill on the outlet of Barrett Pond, which was once known as "Cole's Pond." His sons, Daniel and Elisha III, later built a mill on the West Branch of the Croton River and, as noted by Pelletreau, *"at which a large business for those times was carried on. Connected with the grist mill was a saw and fulling mill, and to the latter, cloth of the good honest homespun of former days was brought from far and near"* (677). This farm, along with the mills, was passed down to subsequent generations of the Cole family until New York City annexed the water supply and purchased their land to build the West Branch Reservoir.

Elisha and his wife, Hannah Smalley Cole, who were married in Massachusetts in 1739, had twelve children, with three of the boys (Ebenezer, Daniel and Nathan) becoming Baptist preachers like their father. They all served at the Mt. Carmel Baptist Church in Carmel, and are buried in the church cemetery. Daughter Priscilla married Gen. James Townsend, who purchased a 352-acre tract located on the top and northwestern side of the mountain.

Just a little east of Coles Mills stood the Hopkins family farm, house and inn, consisting of 341 acres purchased from the Commissioners of Forfeiture. Captain Solomon Hopkins was a patriot during the Revolution, and was the brother-in-law of "The Spy," Enoch Crosby (Solomon was married to

Enoch's sister, Elizabeth). Crosby was once fired at through the window by an unknown assailant, with the ball grazing his neck and shirt collar. A second midnight attack occurred in which Hopkins and Crosby were nearly beaten to death, and the house pillaged. Their neighbors, hearing the commotion, chased down the Tories, catching up with them on the bank of the Croton River, and dispatched them with extreme prejudice (Barnum). The Hopkins could trace their lineage back to Stephen Hopkins, who came to the New World on the Mayflower. Their son Reuben reportedly died in 1798 by drowning in a tanning vat, while their grandson Solomon served during the War of 1812. Their great-grandson, Addison J. Hopkins, was an attorney and served during the Civil War.

Family farming required the proper mix of male and female family members in order to ensure enough labor for the various tasks needed to be performed. For this reason, it was common for family members to be periodically "loaned" from one farm to another to maintain the proper balance and ensure a succession of experienced farm hands from one generation to the next. As the children grew into adulthood, they would typically marry within the closed-knit community of neighbors, common schools and houses of worship. Every early family became inter-related to nearly every other family over time. Multiple generations of inter-related family members commonly lived under one roof. For all these reasons, determining the succession of farm ownership over time can be a very confusing and daunting task, especially when performed 200-plus years after the fact.

Every April, the practice of farm and field rotation would occur in which family members of one farm location would move to another family farm to take advantage of the best farm production opportunities available.

Life on a farm in these times was not an easy one, especially for those in the rock-laden hills and valleys of Mt. Nimham. The soil in this area was not very fertile; a farmer could grow subsistence crops and perhaps a little more, but could not thrive and accumulate money. Instead, these farmers focused more on raising oxen, cattle, horses, pigs, sheep and chickens, cleared fields for grazing and subsistence crops, harvested apples for cider, sold timber for lumber and railroad ties, created charcoal from the burning of green wood in large pits, and the more skillful created wood cabinets and furniture. At first, farmers focused on raising cattle, but eventually dairy and sheep farming would dominate the area until the very early 1900s. On some of the steeper slopes, including much of the mountain, sheep farming was very popular, especially during time periods such as the Civil War, when wool was greatly in demand with the absence of cotton from the South. However, the sheep market was prone to both boom and bust periods, and when the market collapsed in the 1830s, many farmers left this area and moved to the new territories in Michigan and Wisconsin.

As fields were cleared, stones were gathered to form the stone fences we see today that originally served to mark off and separate fields and property lines. As the proverb goes, "good fences make good neighbors," and those appointed as "fence viewers" made sure these fences met the standards of the day. Agricultural fields were marked off in a square or rectangular shape. The fences were intended to keep animals within their confines, and to keep animals out of the crop fields. Ledge fences were built along steep ridge lines to keep the animals from tumbling over the edge, and wetland fences kept them from being stuck in the mud and fouling the water. Stone fences are also commonly found along the old roadways to allow unencumbered passage.

It's hard to imagine today, but by the mid-1800s most of the woodland trees had been cleared and harvested. By necessity, roads were cleared and maintained by the "path masters" to allow for the transport of materials to the mills, and for travel purposes to and from neighbors' farms, family, and church. Many of the early roads were originally Native American Indian trails left by the Nochpeem, and reused by the early settlers. Throughout the 19th century, milk production became an increasingly popular activity, peaking around 1900. After dairy farming fell into decline in the early 1900s, the remaining farmers grew apples, raised poultry, and sold eggs for a living.

The typical colonial farmhouse was scantily furnished. It was solidly built of wood, but the builders gave all too little attention to comfort, and the average farmhouse would have been scarcely endurable in winter but for the great open wood-fire about which the family (usually a large one) gathered in the evening and made brooms, shelled nuts, and told stories. It was typical for extended families to live under one roof, representing several generations. There were few "manufactories," so the people supplied many of their own wants. Nearly every farmer was also a rudimentary mechanic. He and his sons usually made the furniture for the household and many of the implements of the farm as well, while his wife and daughters spun the flax and wove it into a coarse cloth from which the family was clothed. The men hunted for their meat and cut down trees for firewood. The women made soaps and candles.

Sundays were always reserved for church services, and most of the early settlers were Baptists. Residents of the Mt. Nimham area attended either the First Baptist Church of Kent Cliffs (originally located where Boyd's

Reservoir is located, and later moved to the hillside above the reservoir), or the Kent & Fishkill Baptist Church at Farmers Mills. A few others, including the Cole family, attended the Mt. Carmel Baptist Church in Carmel.

In addition to the house in which the family lived, each farm usually contained a barn, a smokehouse and a woodhouse. Many farms also included root cellars, or what are generically known as "stone chambers" today (see Appendix G). The typical home was built of either stone, wooden planks or bricks, usually consisting of one large room. Other rooms would be added as the family grew. The large open fireplace would always have a fire burning, winter or summer, for it was difficult to re-light the fire in an age before matches were available. The parents' bed would be located in a corner of the room, with shutters or doors built around it. Above the main room there was a loft used mainly as a bedroom for the older children or for storing provisions. Each night the children would climb a ladder to the loft to go to bed on feather beds and sleep under feather comforters. Younger children slept in trundle beds that were stored under their parents' bed. Elderly family members slept on long cradles near the fire.

Families were large in those days, averaging between five to twelve children. Large families were an economic necessity in order to carry out all the chores needed on the farm just to ensure survival. These early families also had to deal with the heartbreak associated with the nearly inevitable loss of some of their brood, as childhood illnesses could easily become fatal in an era before antibiotics and immunizations. Child birth also posed a significant danger to women of child-bearing age.

The typical day began early for the entire family. At sunrise, the mother and daughters prepared a large breakfast for the family. Dinner was served at midday, with perhaps a snack in the evening. The father and sons planted, tended and harvested crops, cut and chopped wood, cared for the animals, maintained the houses and fences, traded with the local blacksmith for tools, made utensils and furnishings for the home, and took their products to the mills and markets. The primary markets for the Mt. Nimham farmers were the Coles Mills and Farmers Mills communities, although their central location allowed them to also frequent the Ludingtonville and Boyd's Corners communities as well. The mother and daughters cooked, sewed, mended, made candles and spun cloth.

Apples and pumpkins were used for baking and cider. Apple cider was the beverage of choice during these times. Apples were picked in great quantities to be dried and stored, and later made into applesauce. There is continuing evidence of the former orchards along Mt. Nimham Court.

Smoked and dried meats and fish played an important part in their diet. Without refrigeration, smoking and drying were their means of preservation. Many of the corbelled stone chambers we still see today were built by these early farmers to assist in preserving food for themselves and their animals in an age before electricity and refrigeration. During very cold winters, meat would be wrapped in cloth and buried in the grain bin in the barn where they would freeze. Farmers would share a side of beef with their neighbors, who would return the favor at a later time. Squirrels and other small animals would typically come in droves to eat the vegetables, giving the farmers opportunities to shoot them for food. Venison and bear meat were also fairly plentiful in the early years.

One of the cottage industries on Mt. Nimham involved the manufacture of charcoal. Charcoal was produced by placing fresh-cut green wood into a large pit, arranging the wood in a cone-shaped, tee-pee like manner within the pit, igniting the wood and covering it with sod. The smoldering fire would be watched for several days, depending upon the amount being produced. There are numerous old pits found on the top of the mountain where this activity was practiced. It is reported that an individual by the name of "Indian Joe Smalley" was very active in this endeavor on the mountain. Local blacksmiths and foundries were the primary markets for the charcoal that was produced.

In an age before electricity, the amount of ice a farmer could produce and store was considered a measure of their wealth. Many of the stone chambers in this area are in close proximity to water sources, and the farmers would cut the ice into large blocks, and separate these blocks with layers of sawdust. It is believed that many of these chambers were used to store ice, in addition to dairy and food products. For example, the "milk house" located on the Hawkins/Light/Parker/Maynard farm on the northern end of the mountain is positioned directly in front of a man-made pond. The farmers were also known to grow and store mangelwurzels, a large root vegetable of the family Chenopodiaceae, genus *Beta* (beets), developed in the 1700s for use in feeding their livestock (Baker).

Cleanliness, as we know it today, did not exist in those days. In fact, the Native American Indians were appalled by the lack of personal hygiene among the early European settlers. Clothing, mostly made of wool, linen or a combination of the two, was washed only in summer and baths were almost unheard of. Some children were actually sewn into their clothes in the fall, and the clothing was not removed until springtime. Clothes were not removed completely for sleeping. Boots and shoes were removed, and girls took off their long skirts and slept in their petticoats which had blouse-like tops.

Children in this area were generally named after their grandparents and parents. It was common for a male child to be named after his paternal grandfather, and for a female to be named after her maternal grandmother. As the same names were used over and over, nicknames and the use of middle names came into play to differentiate one from the other. Many children of English settlers were given Old Testament Biblical names, such as Elijah, Moses, Jeremiah, Isaiah, Jacob, Ruth, or Esther. Meanwhile, the children of Dutch parents were often named for New Testament figures (MacCracken, 98).

The children played games such as "hide and seek," "blind man's bluff," "rover come over," and "odd and even." Neighbors were usually very cordial with each other. They helped their neighbors with big jobs such as plowing a large field, raising a barn, or building stone fences. These sometimes turned into large social gatherings, with neighbors bringing food for the celebration.

As the years went by, the farms in the Mt. Nimham area were passed down to the descendents of the original settlers. As daughters married, some property eventually transferred to their in-laws. Different sections of farms were sold off to raise money or for barter purposes, and sometimes re-purchased later on. The designation of property boundaries on the early deeds often referred to particular rock formations or specific trees that stood during their days here.

At first, the children were educated at home by their parents or by teachers who traveled from place to place. Eventually, the young boys attended one-room schoolhouses for grades 1 through 8, or until they were old enough to help out full-time on the farm. Finally, the girls joined their brothers in the one-room schoolhouses. The children on the western portion of Mt. Nimham attended school at "School House No. 1", located near Boyd's Corners to the southwest, just north of the "First Kent Baptist Church." For children living on the eastern and southern face of the mountain, Schoolhouse No. 8, located to the south just east of Coles Mills, was their schoolhouse. This was the first schoolhouse established in the town of Kent. Those to the north and northeast attended "School House No. 4," also known as the "Robinsontown School House." This was located at the northeast corner of Schrade Road and Farmer's Mills (or "Robinsontown") Road.

Their teachers were very strict, and concentrated on the alphabet, reading, numbers and manners.

According to Pelletreau, in referring to the Coles farm site on the southern end of Mt. Nimham:

"It was on this farm that the first school house in Kent was built. This stood about eight rods east of the present school house, and was torn down more than sixty years ago. In its place was built another, for which purpose Abraham, Nathaniel, Reuben and Jeremiah Hopkins leased "for one peppercorn, to be paid annually 4 rods square of ground, five rods north westerly of the old school house, and south westerly of Daniel F. Cole's mills for the term of forty years." This in turn became unfit for use and pretty well hacked to pieces by several generations of jack knives, and the present school house was erected, a few rods west of the former one, on land bought from Stephen Townsend, December 15th, 1865, in exchange for the former site" (678).

This schoolhouse, reconstructed in 1865, still stands today at the bottom of Coles Mills Road (see Illustration 6). It was moved from its original location, just west of Smokey Hollow Court, to the bottom of Coles Mills Road, and is now a private residence.

Illustration 6: Schoolhouse No. 8, Coles Mills, c. 1865, now a private residence (*Photo by author*)

The residents of Mt. Nimham were deeply involved in the civic affairs of the Town of Kent. Throughout the years, they served as "Path Masters," "Highway Overseers," "Pound Keepers," "Fence Viewers," Supervisor, Constable, Sheriff, and Commissioner of Schools. It was also reported that the patriot James Smalley served as sheriff in the early days following the War of Independence, before the split-off of Putnam from Dutchess County.

The early records of the Town of Frederick/Kent show the names of the following Mt. Nimham area residents serving in various civic positions as follows:

Path Masters: Joseph Cole, Daniel Cole, Milton Dean, Isaiah Hopkins, Philips Smith, Joseph Hopkins, Robert Russell, James Russell, John Wixon, General James Townsend, Solomon Hopkins, Lt. Thomas Russell, Rev. Elisha Cole Jr., Ebenezer Brown, Zachariah Smalley, Joshua Townsend, Lt. Col. Elijah Townsend, Stephen Townsend, John Russell, Henry Light, Stephen Russell, Daniel Brown, Aaron Brown, James Smalley, Isaac Smalley, Morris Russell, Isaac Smalley Jr., Samuel Smalley, Howard Tompkins, and William A. Northrup;

Highway Commissioners: Daniel Cole, Asbury Charles Townsend, Stephen Townsend;

Assessors: Daniel Cole, William A. Northrup;

Fence Viewers: Solomon Hopkins;

Constables: Solomon Hopkins, John Wixon;

Pound Keepers: Solomon Hopkins;

Justices: Stephen Townsend, Coleman Townsend.

The recorded lists of the Road Masters and Path Masters often included notations indicating that a man would be allocated "a day's wages" to be attributed to his tax obligation.

Local residents were also charged a "dog tax," which was entered into a general fund to compensate farmers for the loss of livestock due to dog attacks. This amounted to approximately $.50 per year.

"Fence Viewers" performed a very necessary service in ensuring that the farmers' fences were sound and met a required height, usually about four and one-half feet high, to prevent their animals from wandering into their neighbors' fields and wreaking havoc with crops and other animals. Since most of the fences we see today do not meet this height requirement, the farmers would have used wooden logs and poles to supplement the height of the stone fences.

Some local residents were also involved in the mining of minerals and building materials in the area. General James Townsend, one of the original owners on Mt. Nimham following the confiscation of the loyalist property in Lot No. 5, mined the mountain and later was involved in the Tilly Foster Mine, starting around 1810. He owned a forge, for smelting iron ore, which was located at the northwestern corner of what is now Boyd's Reservoir, along the inlet of the West Branch of the Croton River (Flato, 69-70). Evidence of the Townsend family's mining activities on the mountain still abound.

Brown's Quarry, located on the lower eastern face of Mt. Nimham, just south of Mt. Nimham Court, was a great source of quality serpentine rock (see Illustration 7). Owned by the Brown family (Ebenezer, Aaron, Stephen, and Daniel), it yielded large blocks of high quality ornamental marble that were excavated from this site. As described by William Blake in his "History of Putnam County," published in 1849:

"Another locality, one that has already attracted much notice, is Brown's quarry, near Pine Pond in this county, four or five miles from Carmel village, and one and one quarter miles north northwest of the county poor house. It (the serpentine) is dark colored, dark green to black, and from compact to a coarse crystalline, like coarse-grained hornblende rock. It is granularly foliated, like common white marble, polishes well, and is perfectly black when polished. It may be obtained in large blocks for sawing into slabs. Large slabs lie on the surface in Brown's lot, and the rock is seen in place all around the hill. In the mine lot adjacent, good blocks may probably be obtained by quarrying. Twenty-five to thirty acres of ground are underlaid by this rock on the hillside, west of the brook, which is the outlet of Pine Pond. It is easily accessible, and about one hundred feet above the water level of the adjacent valley. Blocks of many tons' weight can be easily procured; in fact, many of this size are now lying on the surface, and require no blasting or splitting before they are put in the saw-mill. Magnetic oxide of iron, or chromate of iron, is disseminated through the serpentine in some parts of the serpentine bed; and this variety of the rock will not be suitable to work, as it can neither be sawed nor polished easily. The quarry seems to be sufficient to supply the market, not only of our own country, but the world, with this kind of ornamental marble, for a long time. It is really a beautiful

material when polished, and it is hoped that it will be extensively used. I have seen no other locality where such a material can be obtained in so large blocks, sound and free from seams and cracks. A marble of this kind was used in ancient times, in some of the old Spanish palaces, but it is exceedingly rare in Europe" (35-36).

Another mine, primarily used to excavate arsenic, is located just north of the Brown's Quarry site. On the 1854 R.F. O'Connor Map, it is labeled as the "Silver Mine Hole." The ore that looked like silver, and which attracted many speculators and stockholders, was largely arsenic. Arsenical ore was used in the manufacture of shot, flint, glass and medicinal preparations. However, the only refinery where arsenic could be liberated successfully was located in England. So, over time, the mine fell into disuse and disrepair (Blake; 1854 O'Connor Map of Kent).

The less fortunate inhabitants of this area were supported by the County Alms House and Farm, located on Gipsy Trail Road where the Putnam County Veteran's Park stands today. Some of the residents were buried in the small cemetery located next to Gipsy Trail Road. A few of the local residents

Illustration 7: Portion of "Brown's Quarry" (*Photo by author*)

from the Mt. Nimham area served as "Overseer of the Poor," including Isaac Brown (1843) and Isaac Parker (1885).

To the south of the County Farm, on the road to Carmel at the corner of Nichols Street, was the house of the William Durrell Northrup family for many years in the late 1800s. Known as "Durrell," Mr. Northrup was an attorney practicing in Carmel. According to Pelletreau, on this property was the house that was reported to be the birthplace of Daniel Drew, whose father, Gilbert Drew, owned it. Upon further examination, it appears that the house was actually located in what is now "Reservoir D", on the southeastern end of the Nichols Street causeway that spans across the reservoir. Daniel Drew was credited for creating the phrase "water stock," which was a very popular term in olden days to describe the enhancement of the weight of farm stock for sale by feeding them salt and having them drink an excessive amount of water to artificially increase their weight at the time of sale. After Gilbert Drew passed away, Gen. James Townsend owned this homestead for a time in the early 1800s (690). Daniel Drew later founded the brokerage firm of Drew, Robinson & Company in 1844, and also helped establish the Drew Methodist Church and the Drew Seminary, both in Carmel.

The farmers on Mt. Nimham were able to enjoy the stunning views of the countryside that the mountain afforded them. They could watch the shadow of the mountain extend over the western side as the sun rose, and later across the eastern valley as the sun set. As we enjoy these same magnificent views today, we can only imagine all the hopes, dreams, joys and heartaches of these early inhabitants of the mountain that accompanied the great natural beauty that abounds.

Chapter 5

Mount Nimham in the 19th Century

As the new nation born of revolution entered its infancy, the ancient inhabitants of the Mount Nimham area would not share in the bounty that was to come. The last remaining Nochpeem in Putnam County would be forced out of this area by 1812. Their trail of tears would take them first to Kent, Connecticut, and then on to Stockbridge, Massachusetts. From there, they would be scattered to the wind, with some joining with the Oneida, while others merged with the Pompano in New Jersey. The European transplants would continue to take their place on these lands, mining the mountain, clearing trees for their farms, and forever transforming the landscape. Even with the Revolution behind them, they would still face great challenges of their own in answering the call to arms to preserve the fragile union they had forged . . .

1800: The Federal Census of 1800 displayed the following families in the Mt. Nimham area:

Head of Household	M under 10	M 10 thru 15	M 16 thru 25	M 26 thru 44	M 45+	F under 10	F 10 thru 15	F 16 thru 25	F 26 thru 44	F 45+
Daniel Brown	2			1		3			1	
Ebenezer Brown	2		3		1	1		2		1
Peter Brown	1			1		1			1	
Daniel Cole	1	1	1		1	2	3	1		1
Samuel Hawkins			1	1			1		1	
David Hopkins	2			1				1		
Isaiah Hopkins	1				1					1
James Russell	2		2	1		3	3		1	
Thomas Russell			2	1	1	1		1	1	1
Isaiah Smalley	2	1		1		1			1	
James Smalley				1				1		1
Zachariah Smalley	2	1	2	1		1	1	2		1
Charles Sturdevant	2		1					1		
Eber Townsend		2	1		1	4	1		1	

1801: It is believed that the patriot Rev. Elisha Cole Jr., the founder of Coles Mills, at the age of 82 passed away in this year, and was buried on the family farmstead. His son, Daniel, inherited the old homestead and mills.

1806: The patriot James Russell, an original tenant farmer on Mt. Nimham on Coles Mills Road, passed away in this year at the age of 56. His wife, Elizabeth Light Russell, had predeceased him the year before. Their son Morris, then three years old, would eventually own the Russell family farm on Coles Mills Road on the southern section of Mt. Nimham, heading toward the Philipstown Turnpike, or what is now Route 301.

1808: It was reported that Joseph Light built a stone chamber/root cellar on Cole Shears Road in this year. There are two chambers on that road, so it is not certain which chamber he was involved in building. Joseph Light was the maternal grandfather of the late Ken Townsend.

1809: John Jacob Astor, the famous multi-millionaire of the time, purchased the rights of the heirs of Mary Philipse Morris to their eventual inheritance of the land in Lot No. 5 of the Philipse Patent, which included Mt. Nimham. According to Smith, the original land patents granted to the Philipses included *". . . water, lakes, ponds, pools, pits, quarries, mines, and minerals (gold and silver excepted) . . ."* (42). Astor focused his claim upon the underground mineral deposits. More recent research also suggests that the Commissioners of Forfeiture had failed to account for the lake beds, and had failed to properly sell these off to the tenant farmers (Pelletreau; and Kent Historical Society).

1810: The First Baptist Church of Kent Cliffs was constituted on October 4, 1810, with early meetings held at the residence of Isaac Drew. The first meeting house was built in 1831 near Boyd's Corners. Mt. Nimham-area residents such as James C. Smalley and James J. Townsend would eventually be licensed to preach there. When New York City built the reservoir at Boyd's Corners, the church property was condemned, and a new site was donated by Platt Parker. This was dedicated on September 19, 1869. The property eventually passed into private hands. The original church cemetery, having been moved from what was to become the reservoir, was relocated to the hillside above the foundation of the old church building on Route 301, across from the reservoir. Unfortunately, many of the gravestones have been hauled away and used as foundation stones and doorsteps, but many stones still remain intact (Behr, 82).

The 1810 Federal Census listed the following families in the Mt. Nimham area:

Head of House	M under 10	M 10 thru 15	M 16 thru 25	M 26 thru 44	M 45+	F under 10	F 10 thru 15	F 16 thru 25	F 26 thru 44	F 45+
Aaron Brown	2	2		1				1	1	
Daniel Brown	1	2		1		2	1	2	1	
Ebenezer Brown					1					1
Stephen Brown	3			1		2	1		1	
Daniel Cole		1	1		1		2			1
Daniel Cole Jr.	1		1		1			1		1
Jesse Cole	2			1				1		
David Hopkins	2	1		1		2			1	
Isaiah Hopkins			1		1					1
James Russell	2	1		1		1			1	
Thomas Russell			1	1	1	1				1
Isaiah Smalley		2			1	2	1			1
Isaac Smalley	4			1		2		1		
James Smalley					1					1
James Smalley 2nd			1						1	
Zachariah Smalley		2			1			1		1
Zachariah Smalley 2nd	2		1					1		
Elijah Townsend		1			1					1
Joshua Townsend		1	1		1	1		1		
James Townsend	4		·	1			1		1	
Gen James Townsend	1	1	1		1		1	1		1
James Townsend Jr.		1	1			1		1		
Melanson Townsend	1			1		3			1	

1811: Following the death of the patriot Chief Daniel Nimham and his brave warriors in 1778, the remnants of the Wappinger had mostly scattered to other tribes in Connecticut, Massachusetts, upstate New York and New

Jersey. The very last remaining band in Putnam County had settled on a tract of land in the northern portion of Kent, near Sagamore Lake. As described by Pelletreau in 1886: *"A small band had their dwelling place on a low tract of land by the side of a brook, under a high hill, in the northern part of the town of Kent, but all that remained of them have long sinced passed away, and the place that knew them once will know them no more forever"* (86). 1811 marked the end of any organized settlement of the Wappinger people in our town and county.

Zachariah Smalley, a patriot of the Revolution and the son of the patriot and Mt. Nimham patriarch James Smalley, died on July 15th at the age of 51.

1812: The following residents of the Mt. Nimham area served their country during the War of 1812:

- Elisha Cole IV, the son of the patriot Elisha Cole III and his wife, Charity Hazen Cole, from the southernmost end of Mt. Nimham at Coles Mills;

- Asahel Cole, the son of Joseph and Rebecca Berry Cole, and Elisha IV's first cousin, also from the Coles Mills area;

- Jesse Cole, first cousin of Elisha IV and Asahel, and the son of the patriot Deacon Daniel Cole;

- Solomon Hopkins, the son of the patriot Jeremiah Hopkins and the grandson of the patriot Captain Solomon Hopkins.

On September 18th, three months after the start of the war, the Mt. Nimham patriot Lt. Col. James Townsend was appointed commander of the militia's 30th Infantry Brigade. He eventually achieved the rank of Brigadier General.

On December 28th, Addison J. Hopkins was born, the son of Solomon Hopkins and the grandson of the patriot Jeremiah Hopkins. Addison was also the great-grandson of the patriot Captain Solomon Hopkins, the brother-in-law of 'The Spy', Enoch Crosby.

Isaac Smalley, the son of the patriot Zachariah Smalley and a farmer on the northwest side of Mt. Nimham, passed away in this year at the early age of 32, just a year after his father's death.

1813: On March 6th, Daniel Brown passed away at the age of 43. He owned the farm just east of Mt. Nimham on Gipsy Trail Road, near where the New

York State Multiple Use Area parking lot is located today. He was laid to rest in the Mt. Carmel Baptist Church Cemetery in Carmel.

1815: The patriot Elder Ebenezer Cole, the son of the patriot Rev. Elisha Cole Jr., died on August 18th at the age of 61. He had followed in his father's footsteps in serving at the Mt. Carmel Baptist Church in Carmel. Ebenezer Cole is buried in the Mt. Carmel Baptist Church Cemetery.

1820: The Federal Census listed the following families in the Mt. Nimham area (on some pages there are missing columns, which are denoted as "N/A"):

Head of House	M under 10	M 10 thru 15	M 16 thru 18	M 16 thru 25	M 26 thru 44	M 45 +	F under 10	F 10 thru 15	F 16 thru 25	F 26 thru 44	F 45 +
Aaron Brown		1	1	3		1			1	1	
Phebe Brown	1	1		2			1	1	2		1
Stephen Brown	1	1			1	1	2	1	2	1	
Daniel Cole						2			1	N/A	N/A
Daniel Cole Jr.	2	1			2		2		N/A	N/A	N/A
Eleazer Cole	1	2		2	0	1	2		1	1	1
Elisha Cole III	1	1			1		1		1	N/A	N/A
Jesse Cole	1	1			1		1	1		N/A	N/A
John Ferris	2				1		1			1	
David Hopkins	1	1		1		1	2	1	2		1
Isaiah Hopkins						1					1
John Russell	1	2		2		1	2	2		N/A	N/A
Stephen Russell		1				1			1		1
Tartulas Russell	2				1		3				1
William Russell	2			1						N/A	N/A
Isaiah Smalley	1					1		1	N/A	N/A	N/A
Isaiah Smalley II	2			1			1		N/A	N/A	N/A
Isaac Smalley				1			1		1		
James Smalley						1			1		1

Head of House	M under 10	M 10 thru 15	M 16 thru 18	M 16 thru 25	M 26 thru 44	M 45 +	F under 10	F 10 thru 15	F 16 thru 25	F 26 thru 44	F 45 +
James Smalley 2nd					1		1		1	N/A	N/A
Joseph Smalley	1		1						N/A	N/A	N/A
Zachariah Smalley II	3	1			1		1			1	
Joseph Smith	1				1		1		N/A	N/A	N/A
Elijah Townsend	1					1	1	N/A	N/A	N/A	N/A
James Townsend	2	4			1				1	1	
Joshua Townsend	2				1		4			1	
Isaac Wixon	3				1		2	1		1	

In this year, Dr. Elias Cornelius, a surgeon from Carmel, donated through his will a 196-acre farm to Putnam County. Located on the southeastern base of Mt. Nimham, this site would become the Putnam County Alms House and Farm. The residents of the Alms House included paupers, orphans, those who were blind, deaf, or insane, and veterans with war disabilities. The residents raised their own vegetables, some livestock, chickens and eggs. The County Farm replaced the previously archaic practice of auctioning the poor to the highest bidder to pay their debts. Today, this is the site of the Putnam County Veteran's Park on Gipsy Trail Road.

1821: Joseph Cole, the son of the patriot Elder Ebenezer Cole from Coles Mills, served as the Sheriff of Putnam County. He was the fifth sheriff in the history of Putnam County.

1822: It is believed that the patriot Ebenezer Brown, age 82, died in this year. Ebenezer and his sons Aaron, Stephen and Daniel, owned several farms on the eastern base of Mt. Nimham, mostly south of Pine Pond except for one parcel owned by Aaron which adjoined the northern end of the lake. The Brown family was also associated with the mine on the southwestern side of Mt. Nimham Court, which became known as "Brown's Quarry." The mine that was located a little further north was known as "Brown's Silver Mine Hole." Stephen Brown took over his father's farm after his passing.

The "Phebe Brown" listed in the 1820 Federal Census was the widow of Daniel Brown. They had a daughter, Abigail (1802-1861), who married Elijah Light. They in turn bore a daughter, Margaret (1834-1874), who married Howard Tompkins (1817-1899). Howard Tompkins was found on the maps of the 1800s as owning the farm just south of Pine Pond on Gipsy Trail Road, and a nearby property on the eastern side of the mountain across from the current NYS DEC parking area on Gipsy Trail Road.

1823: James Smalley, a patriot from the Revolution and an original purchaser of property on Mt. Nimham, died at the age of 88. His will passed all his farmland to his son Isaiah, except for 2 1/2 acres for his grandson, Zachariah Jr., the son of Isaiah's late son, Zachariah Sr. All his personal property was passed equally to his surviving children and to the children of Zachariah (Putnam County Surrogate Court, Will Book "A", #334).

Also in this year, the patriot Lt. Col. Elijah Townsend passed away at the age of 72. He was the patriarch of the Townsend clan located on Mt. Nimham up until the early 1900s. His descendents, who served in numerous civic positions over the years, lived approximately half way up the mountain, on the "Fairview Farm", located at what is now the NYS DEC parking area, at the corner of Mt. Nimham Court and Coles Mills Road.

1826: On February 3rd, the patriot Elisha Cole III passed away at the age of 83. He had served in the Dutchess County Militia, 7th Regiment, under Col. Ludington, and was the son of the patriot Rev. Elisha Cole, Jr. He was buried in the Cole family plot.

1827: After Mary Philipse Morris' death in 1825, John Jacob Astor pursued his claim to certain lands formerly known as part of the Upper Highlands Patent of the Philipse Patent, Lot No. 5, in federal court. Recent research indicates that the issue may have centered around the legal status of the land located under the lakes which the Commissioners of Forfeiture had not fully accounted for. Astor lost this case in court three times, the last being a Supreme Court ruling under Chief Justice John Marshall. But while these cases were underway, the New York Legislature passed an act to extinguish Astor's claim for the sum of $450,000. This settlement was concluded in 1828, and the Mt. Nimham area farmers retained their ownership rights for the lands in question. The fact that Astor was awarded $450,000 has led some previous historians to conclude that he was successful in court, which is not the case (Pelletreau; Kent Historical Society; and Putnam County Historian's Office).

1829: The patriot Jeremiah Hopkins, the son of the patriot Captain Solomon Hopkins from the southern end of Mt. Nimham, passed away on October 17th at the age of 67. He was laid to rest in the Gilead Burial Ground in Carmel.

1830: Stephen Townsend, the son of Joshua and the grandson of the patriot

Lt. Col. Elijah Townsend, married Mary "Polly" Smalley. Polly Smalley was the daughter of Isaac and Elizabeth Russell Smalley, long time residents of the Mt. Nimham area on Smalley Corners Road, and was the granddaughter of the patriot Zachariah Smalley. This marriage brought together three of the stalwart patriot family names who lived on Mt. Nimham: the Townsends, Smalleys and Russells. Stephen and Polly Townsend would make their home on the mountain for the next 63 years, on what was known as "Fairview Farm," where the NYS DEC parking area is located today.

1831: The patriot Deacon Daniel Cole, the son of the patriot Elisha Cole Jr., died on December 10th at the age of 85, and is buried in the Mt. Carmel Baptist Church Cemetery.

1832: General James Townsend, a patriot of the Revolution and the War of 1812, and an original owner of the north-northwestern sides of Mt. Nimham following the Revolution, died on March 13th at the age of 76. In addition to the property on Mt. Nimham, Townsend originally owned the land where the Putnam County Courthouse stands today. Townsend was married to Priscilla Ann Cole, the daughter of the patriot Rev. Elisha Cole Jr. and Hannah Smalley Cole of Coles Mills. He was laid to rest in the Old Baptist Church Cemetery in the Hamlet of Carmel.

1834: On July 17th, the patriot Samuel Hawkins passed away at the age of 74. Hawkins owned two properties, one on the northern end of Mt. Nimham, on what is known today as Maynard Road, or on some maps as "Friend Lane", and the other in Whang Hollow to the east. His nephew, Henry E. Light, would later own the property on the northern end of the mountain itself, which extended to Stockholm Hill. Samuel Hawkins was buried in the Russell-Mead Cemetery.

1835: On May 29th, Berry Cole, the son of the patriot Joseph Cole and the grandson of the patriot Rev. Elisha Cole Jr., passed away at the age of 66. He was laid to rest in the Mt. Carmel Baptist Church Cemetery in Carmel.

1836: Robert W. Russell, the son of the patriot John Russell from Mt. Nimham, served as Supervisor of the Town of Kent until 1838.

1837: On November 1st of this year, Malinda Light (1822-1901), the daughter of John and Elizabeth Light and the sister of Henry E., Moseman B. and Night Light, married Darius Ferris (1812-1891). Darius Ferris can be found on the maps of 1867 and 1876 as residing at the former James D. Hyatt location on Gipsy Trail Road, on the eastern side of Mt. Nimham, at what is now known as the Pine View Farm. His sisters, Sarah Maria and

Susan Jane, married his bothers-in-law, Moseman and Henry Light, respectively.

1838: Farmers Mills was organized by an association of local farmers and merchants. Some of these farmers included members of the Townsend family (Samuel, Warren, Horace, and Samuel A.) from the Townsend Ridge area of Kent. Warren and Samuel were married to Betsey and Hannah Caldwell, respectively, and Samuel A. would marry Angeline Barrett, the daughter of Stevens Russell Barrett. The site was originally known as Milltown from an early mill built on a small stream at the outlet of White Pond.

This was the original town center of Kent, and included a flouring mill, fulling and saw mill, a forge, turning shop, mechanic shop, blacksmith, tanning yard and brickyard. It also included the Putnam County Bank, several stores, a post office, hotel, two taverns, and a branch of the Borden Condensed Milk Company called the Elgin Gilt-Edged Butter and Cheese Factory. This building is now known as the "Rise-Up Fellowship," a Christian academy located on Farmers Mills Road.

Being located on the major east-west thoroughfare then known as the Philipstown Turnpike, and would later become known as Farmers Mills Road, this town center thrived for a number of years. Some of the farmers from the Mt. Nimham area brought their timber, grain, apples and cloth to be processed in these mills. After the building of the Harlem and Hudson River railroads in 1849, which bypassed the Farmers Mills area, the settlement at Farmers Mills eventually became a stranded village and gradually passed into history (Pelletreau, 682-684).

The Mt. Nimham farmers were more likely to avail themselves of the mills at nearby Coles Mills, which included a grist mill, saw mill and fulling mill.

1840s: After steadily increasing over the years, the population of Kent began decreasing in the 1840s (see Appendix B). This was largely due to the collapse of the sheep industry, which had taken on the characteristics of a "boom-bust" market similar to the excesses seen in the financial markets in recent years. Sheep had been introduced around 1809, and the industry had exploded by the 1830s. When the bubble burst, many of these farmers moved westward to the new territories opening up in Michigan and Wisconsin.

1843: In this year, Milton Niles Dean and his family moved to the farm located off of Gipsy Trail Road just south of the County Farm. The anterior portion of their property led up the southeastern side of Mt. Nimham, between the current County Park and the border with Carmel. He was a descendant of William Dean, who came to Frederickstown from Rhode Island during the earliest period of settlement of the town. William married Hannah Smith, and their sons, Ezekial and Caleb, were noted as having been among the earliest taxpayers in Frederickstown (Beers, 1897). The Dean farms were located along Horsepound Road in Kent. "Dean Pond "continues to serve as a reminder of their patriotism and devotion to our town.

Another son, the patriot John Dean, served in the militia during the Revolution. He married Miss Mary Niles, and they had a son, Niles Dean. Niles Dean married Nancy Northrup, the daughter of Stephen Northrup, another patriot from the Revolution. Their son, Milton Niles Dean, was born in 1815, and lived on his father's farm until after the elder's death in 1833. He then moved to Dutchess County, returning to Kent in 1843, where he engaged in farming for the next 50 years. He married Phebe Jane Haviland, and their children were John Haviland Dean, William Niles Dean, Nancy L. Dean and Colonel Fremont Dean.

1845: The 1845 New York State Census listed the following farms in the Mt. Nimham area, along with the number of "improved acres":

- Isaac Smalley - 100 acres
- Henry Light - 50 acres
- Moseman Light - 15 acres
- Marah (Mary) Smalley - 25 acres
- Tebelee McDaniels - 3 acres
- Stephen Brown - 90 acres
- Stephen Townsend - 100 acres
- Morrace (Morris) Russell - 60 acres
- James Smalley - 30 acres
- Darius Ferris - 6 acres
- Elisha J. Cole - 100 acres
- Jesse Cole - 85 acres
- Daniel H. Cole - 55 acres
- Nathaniel Tompkins - 80 acres

For the Town of Kent overall, the census results showed that there were:

- 319 pupils in common schools;
- wheat was grown on only 45 acres;
- corn was grown on 545 acres;
- oats were grown on 402 acres;
- rye was grown on 354 acres;

- buckwheat was grown on 379 acres;
- turnips were grown on 16 acres;
- 146 acres of potatoes;
- 2,567 head of cattle;
- 1,264 cows milked;
- 133,516 lbs of butter produced;
- 1,704 lbs of cheese produced;
- 260 horses;
- 2,181 sheep;
- 3,710 lbs of wool produced;
- 1,967 hogs;
- 5 gristmills;
- 6 sawmills;
- 2 fulling mills;
- 2 carding machines;
- 2 tanneries;
- 3 Baptist churches;,
- 10 common schools;
- 2 inns/taverns;
- 6 retail stores;
- 143 farmers;
- 7 merchants;
- Total population of 1,729.

1846: The following residents of the Mt. Nimham area served their country during the Mexican War:

- Isaac Smalley, from the northwestern base of Mt. Nimham near the corner of Smalley Corners and Maynard/Beach Roads;
- Zachariah Smalley, Isaac Smalley's cousin from the western side of Mt. Nimham;
- Ansel Cole, the son of Joshua Cole and the grandson of the patriot Elisha Cole III, from Coles Mills.

1848: The Hudson River Mining Company operated the mine located about one-half mile southwest of Pine Pond, on the lower eastern face of Mt. Nimham, labeled on town maps as "Brown's Quarry." The ore was taken to the forge formerly owned by Gen. James Townsend, which was located at the northern end of what is now Boyd's Reservoir, on the inlet of the west branch of the Croton River. There, the ore was smelted, and evidence of its existence in the form of tailings and slag may still be found along the banks of the river and on Route 301 in Kent Cliffs. James Townsend was later involved in the extraction and refinement of ores from the Tilly Foster Mine in the years before his death (Flato, 69).

It was also reported during these times that silver was taken from the mine on Smalley Hill known as the "Silver Mine Hole." The 1854 map of Putnam County shows the location of this mine on the eastern face of the mountain, north of Mt. Nimham Court. As reported by Pelletreau below, there was some doubt as to whether the silvery-looking substance found in these mines was actually silver. It is now known that the "silver" was actually arsenical ore. However, the mine proved to be unproductive and was eventually closed. But over time, stories grew and took on a life of their own in the area about silver mines, sparking a great deal of interest and speculation. Many invested as stockholders, inevitably losing their original investments. Later, around the turn of the century, a local mining engineer aroused renewed interest with his analysis showing an abundance of large veins of arsenical iron pyrites. This ore could be used for the extraction of arsenic, which was used in pharmaceuticals, poisons and chemicals. The D.S. Chemical Company re-opened the mine, but the condition of the mine proved to make this a very difficult enterprise. In addition, while the ore was sent to Mamaroneck for smelting, the operation there was not sufficient to successfully extract a refined product. The nearest smelting forge capable of rendering a useful end-product was located in England. Thus, it became impractical to continue the operation, and the mine was finally closed again sometime in the 1917-1918 period (Flato, 70).

In describing the "silver mine," Pelletreau reported: *The shaft is about forty feet deep, and yellow pulverulent sulphuret of arsenic covers the shaft, resulting from the decomposition of the arsenical sulphuret of iron, of which there is evidently a large quantity. The idea that silver exists here is received with doubt"* (703).

1849: Benjamin B. Hopkins, the grandson of the patriot Jeremiah Hopkins, and great-grandson of the patriot Captain Solomon Hopkins, served as the Supervisor of the Town of Kent in this year.

1851: Coleman S. Townsend was born on December 7th, 1851, to Stephen and Mary "Polly" Smalley Townsend of Mt. Nimham. Coleman would later marry Rachel Curry, and they had 3 children: Stephen, Coleman S., and Hamilton Fish Townsend. Coleman Sr. was Justice of the Peace for the Town of Kent for 16 years, and became known as "Judge Townsend." He was also a farmer on Mt. Nimham nearly his entire life, on the family farm appropriately named as the "Fairview Farm." His sons Coleman S., Stephen and Hamilton would carry on the family farming tradition on the old homestead. Stephen would eventually live on what is now called Clear Pool Road. He was a miner and stone mason, and two of his sons carried on in that trade. The Townsends constructed the explosives bunker found near the DEC parking area on Mt. Nimham to store the munitions needed to dislodge the desired materials used in their trade.

In this year, a fire at Coles Mills, then owned by Daniel H. Cole, the son of the patriot Deacon Daniel Cole, destroyed the woodhouse, and a storehouse, causing damage totaling approximately $800 (Putnam County Courier).

1852: James C. Smalley, the son of Zachariah and Priscilla Odell Smalley, and grandson of the patriot Zachariah Smalley, was ordained to preach at the First Baptist Church of Kent in this year, then located near Boyd's Corners. He continued to preach until he resigned in 1869 (Pelletreau, 680).

Stephen Brown, the son of Ebenezer Brown and the owner of a farm south of Pine Pond extending to the eastern side of Mt. Nimham, died at the age of 73 on April 20th and is buried in the Kent Cliffs Baptist Church Cemetery. Included in his property holdings was "Brown's Quarry," located on the lower eastern side of Mt. Nimham. His heirs, including his sister Mahala Brown Russell (the wife of Morris Russell), and his son Stephen, took ownership of his property following his passing.

1853: Coleman R. Shear was born in January of 1853, the son of Daniel B. and Martha A. Shear. Around 1883, he married Ellen E. Smalley, the daughter of Isaac and Esther Smalley. They lived on the western access road leading up to Mt. Nimham, which was then known as "Shear's Road." This road would later become known as "Cole Shear's Road," and is now called "Cole Shears Court."

1854: Stephen Brown, the son of Stephen and grandson of the patriot Ebenezer Brown, passed away on April 23rd, and is buried in the First Baptist Church of Kent Cliffs Cemetery. He owned the farm just up the hill from the Stephen Townsend farm, where a stone chamber still stands today, along with the stone fences outlining the approach to his house. He was just 32 years of age.

The R.F. O'Connor Map of Putnam County (see Illustration 8), published in this year, showed three farms owned by the Smalleys (Mrs. Smalley, Isaac, and Zachariah), along with the Stephen Townsend, the Stephen Brown estate, and Morris Russell family farms on Mt. Nimham, which was then known as "Smalley Hill." Sandwiched between the Smalley farms, on Cole Shear's Road, was the farm of John Wixon (the son of Peleg Wixon). At the

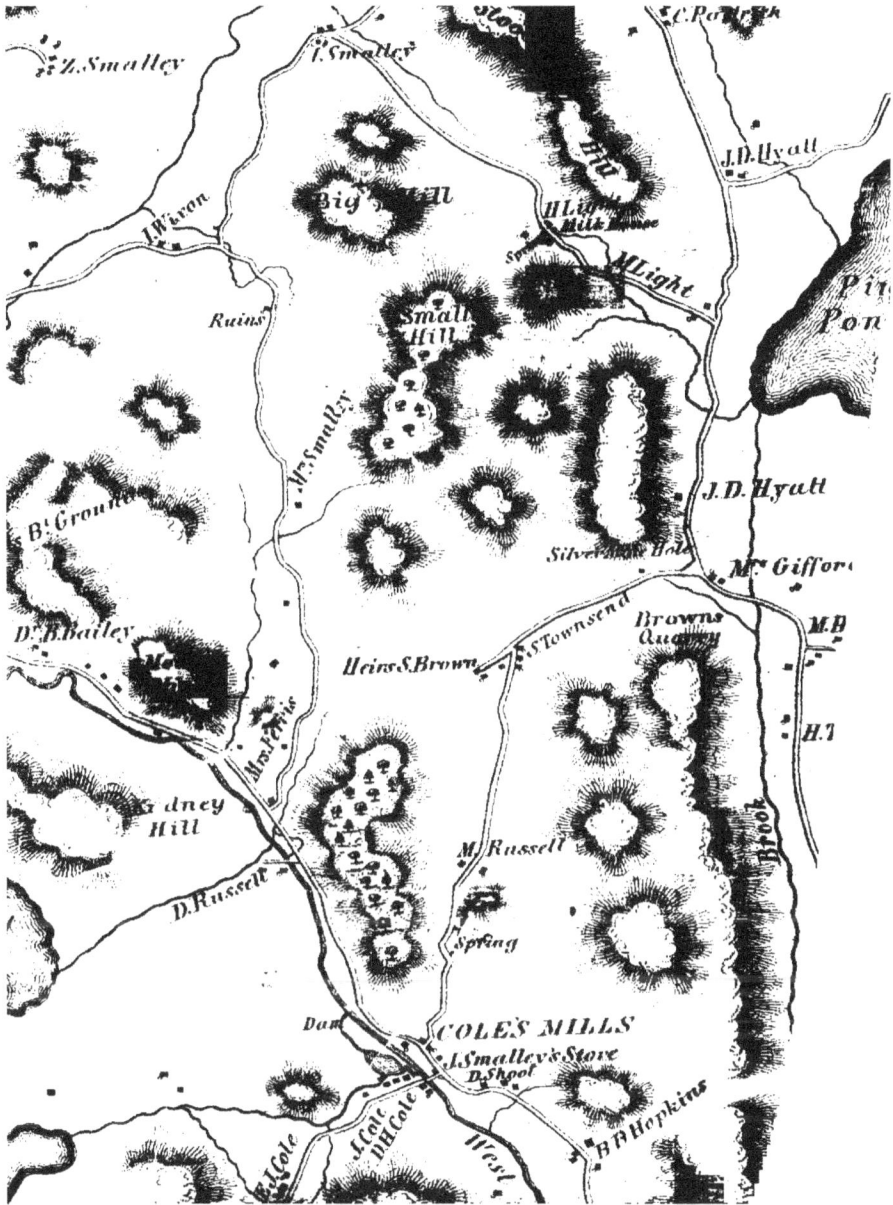

Illustration 8: Mt. Nimham Area Excerpt of the 1854 R.F. O'Connor Map of Kent *(Courtesy of the Putnam County Historian's Office)*

bottom of Cole Shears Road was found the farm of Joshua Smalley, the son of Zachariah II, and the brother of Rev. James C. and Nathan C. Smalley.

The widow Smalley, located on what is now called Clearpool Road, had been married to Samuel Smalley. They lived on the western side of the mountain in a classic log cabin/carriage house with a large stone fireplace at the end of the cabin. This treasure is still standing, and is located adjacent to the Clearpool Education Center.

The 1854 map also shows a location labeled as "Ruins" off of Cole Shears and Clear Pool Road, on the western side of Mt. Nimham. An inspection of this site has resulted in the identification of a stone chamber at this location, with its opening facing east toward the western wall of the mountain. This curious designation on the map raises some questions regarding these chambers, which are found throughout Kent and Putnam County, and are discussed in greater detail in Appendix G following this timeline.

According to this map, James D. Hyatt, the husband of Minerva Mead (Moses F. Mead's sister), was listed at the location eventually occupied by Erastus Smalley, at the very end of the original Whang Hollow Road at the intersection with Gipsy Trail Road. Moseman Light was shown at the current Gipsy Trail administration building location. Henry Light was found a little to the west of his brother, Moseman, on the northern side of the mountain, and the map made note of a "milk house" on his farm, which is the site of another corbelled stone chamber. This farm was originally owned by the patriot Samuel Hawkins, who was Henry and Moseman Light's uncle.

"Mrs. Gifford" (Polly) is found on the farm just south of Pine Pond on Gipsy Trail Road. A little further south, on the western side of the road, was the farm of Howard Tompkins.

Next to Tompkins, to the south, at the location previously owned by the Browns and later by Jeremiah Mead, which is now the NYS Ranger station, the map showed Moseman B. Hyatt. He was the son of James D. Hyatt, from further north on the corner of Gipsy Trail and Whang Hollow Road.

1856: Isaiah Smalley, a patriot from the Revolution and son of the patriot James Smalley, died on July 7th at the age of 100 years, 3 months, and 14 days. Being the eldest son of James Smalley, he had inherited his father's farm on Mt. Nimham following the elder's death in 1823. Isaiah Smalley was the last surviving Mt. Nimham patriot from the War of Independence, and he is buried in the First Baptist Church of Kent Cliffs Cemetery (Pelletreau, 680).

Also in this year, Addison J. Hopkins, Esq., the son of the patriot Jeremiah Hopkins and grandson of the patriot Captain Solomon Hopkins, served as the Supervisor of the Town of Kent. He lived on the old Hopkins homestead, located on the southeastern base of the mountain.

It was around this time that Stephen Townsend purchased another farm near Coles Mills. However, this property was eventually purchased by New York City as part of its watershed and reservoir program. The Townsends then moved back to the family homestead on Mt. Nimham (Obituary of Coleman S. Townsend, Putnam County Courier).

Also in 1856, Colonel Fremont Dean was born to parents Milton Niles Dean and his wife, Phebe Jane Haviland Dean. He was named for the Mexican War hero, scientist and explorer Colonel John C. Fremont, who was also a noted abolitionist of his day. Colonel's elder brothers were William Niles Dean and John Haviland Dean.

1858: Joshua Townsend, the son of the patriot Lt. Col. Elijah Townsend, and the husband of Ada Russell Townsend, passed away on November 9th at the age of 70. He was laid to rest in the First Baptist Church of Kent Cliffs Burial Ground. Ada Russell was the granddaughter of the patriot Lt. Thomas Russell, whose farm adjoined the Townsend's Fairview Farm on "the road to Coles Mills" or Coles Mills Road. Joshua was survived by his wife, and his son, Stephen Townsend, who would continue living and working on the Fairview Farm on Mt. Nimham for the next 35 years.

1860: The Federal Census of 1860 listed the following families and farms on and around Mt. Nimham:

- Stephen Townsend, farmer, age 49, real estate value of $3,000; wife Polly, age 49; Julia A., age 23; Orvilla, age 20; Freeman, age 18; Augustus, age 15; Coleman, age 8; Sarah M. Frost, age 13;
- James Smalley, age 75, real estate value of $3,300; his wife Phebe, age 46; Emeline, age 18; James K., age 12; Christina, age 8;
- Morris Russell, age 57, real estate value of $2,000; wife Mahala, age 59; Emiline, age 30; Harriet, age 28; Perris, age 26;
- Isaac Smalley, age 60, real estate value of $7,000; wife Esther, age 60; Warren, age 38; Clarisa, age 37; Louisa, age 28; Isaac, age 22; Elizabeth, age 20; Ellen, age 7; James Saterla, age 10, Abigail Russell, age 80;
- Henry Light, age 54, real estate value of $4,500; wife Susan J., age 41; Harvey E., age 21; Phebe A. Smalley, age 18; Sarah J. Light, age 9;
- Zachariah Smalley, age 71, real estate value of $5,500; wife Persilla, age 75; Abel, age 44; Juliette, age 35; Rosetta, age 6; Emily S., age 3; Zachariah, age 2;
- Joshua Smalley, age 36, real estate value of $3,000; wife Caroline,

age 36; Augustus B., age 11; Euphema L., age 9; Robert D., age 8; Jerard J., age 5; Charles, age 2;

- James C. Smalley, Baptist Clergyman, age 46, real estate value of $4,000; wife Elizabeth, age 43; George, age 18; William, age 16; Emily, age 14; Persilla, age 12; Caroline, age 10; Neumann, age 7; Mary J., age 4; Lenna, age 2;
- Erastus Smalley, age 28, real estate value of $3,500; wife Keturah, age 26; Emily F., age 4;
- Moseman Light, age 43, real estate value of $2,000; Sarah M., age 35; William, age 18; Susan, age 15; Joseph, age 10; Alanson, age 9;
- Wright Wixon, age 37, real estate value of $2,800; Sarah, age 28; Harvey, age 49; Fanny, age 28;
- Mary Smalley, age 60, real estate value of $700; Samuel, age 40; Squire, age 30; Coleman, age 22;
- Polly Gifford, age 60, real estate value $2,000; Ladesca, age 24; Van Rensalaer, age 22;
- Darius Ferris, age 40, real estate value $1,600; Malinda, age 35; Darius Jr., age 18; Rosannah, age 10;
- Harmon Cole, age 47, real estate value $10,000; Julia, age 43; Charles E., age 13; Asenith Barrett, age 24;
- Jesse Cole, age 76, real estate value $5,000; Norman, age 38; Rachael, age 47; Louisa, age 27; Ann Tompkins, age 33; Henry Tompkins, age 3;
- Addison J. Hopkins, age 48, real estate value of $8,500; Louise M. age 29; Eugene B., age 4; Phebe, age 2 months; Betsy (domestic), age 17; Harry Smalley (laborer), age 28.

1861-1865: Ten members of the Smalley family from Putnam County served in the Civil War. Those from the Mt. Nimham area included:

- Riley Smalley, the son of Zachariah and Priscilla O'Dell Smalley (first cousin of William D., uncle of Isaiah, James and Joseph);
- Isaiah Smalley, 16th NY Heavy Artillery, Co. B (first cousin of James and Joseph, nephew of Riley);
- James E. Smalley, 6th NY Heavy Artillery, Co. L (first cousin of Isaiah and Joseph, nephew of Riley);
- Joseph J. Smalley, 6th NY Heavy Artillery, Co. G (first cousin of Isaiah and James, nephew of Riley);
- William D. Smalley, 6th NY Heavy Artillery, Company G, the son of Joseph and Elizabeth Hagar Smalley (first cousin of Riley, second cousin to Isaiah, Joseph and James);
- William D. Smalley, the son of Rev. James C. Smalley and his wife,

Elizabeth Wright Smalley, served in Company G of the 150th N.Y. Infantry;

- John L. Smalley, 6th NY Heavy Artillery, Co. G;
- Garrett D. Smalley, the son of John and Euphemia Smalley.

Others from the Mt. Nimham area included:

- John Haviland Dean, 59th NY Infantry Regiment, Company I, the great-grandson of the patriot John Dean;
- William Niles Dean, 59th NY Infantry Regiment, Company I, also the great-grandson of the patriot John Dean, and younger brother of John Haviland Dean;
- William D. Light, 6th NY Heavy Artillery, Company G, the son of Moseman Light;
- Sgt. Isaac W. Parker, 6th NY Heavy Artillery, Company G, the grandson of John Parker (veteran of the War of 1812) and great-grandson of Nathaniel (a patriot from the Revolution);
- Daniel Webster Cole, grandson of the patriot Deacon Daniel Cole, great-grandson of the patriot Elisha Cole Jr., 176th Regiment, New York Infantry, Company B;
- Charles E. Cole, the son of Ogden and Sarah White Cole, and the great-grandson of the patriot Deacon Daniel Cole, 176th Regiment, New York Infantry, Company E;
- Henry Clay Cole, the son of Allen and Susan E. Cole, and the great-grandson of the patriot Deacon Daniel Cole;
- Addison J. Hopkins, Esq., the grandson of the patriot Jeremiah Hopkins and great-grandson of the patriot Captain Solomon Hopkins.

In addition, it was reported that "Indian Joe Smalley," a Wappinger descendant, served as a scout in the Civil War. He was reportedly a caretaker of a tenant farm, and produced charcoal on Mt. Nimham (Greenwood).

On November 23rd, the 59th NY Infantry Regiment (including John Haviland Dean and his brother, William Niles Dean) disembarked from New York to Washington D.C. There they served under General Wadsworth's command in defense of the nation's capital until January 1862.

It should be noted that the 6th NY Heavy Artillery Regiment, despite its moniker, actually functioned as an infantry unit.

With the South withholding cotton from the North, sheep farming gained in popularity on Mt. Nimham and throughout this area as demand increased for wool to clothe Union troops during the war, and to make up for the shortage of cotton required by the rest of the populace.

1862: John Haviland Dean (see Illustration 9), the son of Milton and Phebe Haviland Dean, died on January 25th from measles at Camp Good Hope, Washington DC. He was 19 years old, and is buried in the Raymond Hill Cemetery. He was the first casualty of the Civil War from the Carmel-Kent area. The Dean family originally owned a farm on Horsepound Road (adjacent to "Dean Pond"), and later moved to the southern portion of Gipsy Trail Road, just south of Nichols Street. Their farm extended up the south-eastern side of Mt. Nimham. The Dean Pond location was the farm where his grandfather, the patriot John Dean, had lived and died. John Haviland Dean's younger brother, William Niles Dean (see Illustration 9), participated in the battles of Harrison's Landing, Malvern Hill, the Second Battle of Bull Run, and South Mountain.

But September 17th marked a milestone in the remarkable story of William Niles Dean, age 18. On September 16th Maj. Gen. George B. McClellan confronted Lee's Army of Northern Virginia at Sharpsburg, Maryland. To Northerners, it was known as the Battle of Antietam. At dawn on September 17th, General Hooker's corps mounted a powerful assault on Lee's left flank that began the single bloodiest day in American military history. Attacks and counterattacks swept across Miller's cornfield and fighting swirled around the Dunker Church. Union assaults against the Sunken Road eventually pierced the Confederate center, but the Federal advantage was not followed up. Late in the day, Burnside's corps finally got into action, crossing the stone bridge over Antietam Creek and rolling up the Confederate right. At a crucial moment, Confederate General A.P. Hill's division arrived from Harpers Ferry and counterattacked, driving back Burnside and saving the day for Lee. Although outnumbered two-to-one, Lee had committed his entire force, while McClellan sent in less than three-quarters of his army, enabling Lee to fight the Federals to a standstill. During the night, both armies consolidated their lines. In spite of crippling casualties, Lee continued to skirmish with McClellan throughout the 18th, while removing his wounded south of the river.

McClellan did not renew the assaults. After dark, Lee ordered the battered Army of Northern Virginia to withdraw across the Potomac into the Shenandoah Valley.

On September 17th, Private William Niles Dean was severely wounded during the Battle of Antietam. He lost part of his jaw, making speech very difficult, and also suffered damage to his spine. According to Beers, *"William Niles Dean was shot in the left cheek, with the ball passing through his face and coming out in front of his right ear, in its course carrying away the left upper jaw, tearing through the roof of his mouth, and carrying away a portion of the right upper jaw, and also a piece of the right lower jaw."*

He was confined to the hospital in Washington D.C. for three months, and from there was discharged, *"and returned home, where he has remained an invalid ever since"* (Beers). A striking figure before the war, William Niles Dean would never marry after returning home. But he eventually became an expert fruit farmer on and around Mt. Nimham. His sister, Nancy, would assist in his recovery by staying at his side for the next 50 years.

Antietam was the bloodiest single day battle in the history of the U.S., with over 23,000 men killed or wounded. This amounts to about nine times the

Illustration 9: William Niles Dean (l.), and his elder brother, John Haviland Dean (r.) *(Courtesy of the Kent Historical Society)*

losses suffered on D-Day during World War II. In fact, there were more deaths on this single day than the total number of deaths of all Americans in the Revolutionary War, the War of 1812, the Mexican War, and Spanish-American War, combined.

The Union's strategic victory at Antietam thwarted Southern General Robert E. Lee's plans to invade the North, which he had hoped would force President Lincoln into agreeing to peace terms. Emboldened by this victory, President Lincoln issued the Emancipation Proclamation, freeing the slaves. This forced both England and France to cancel any plans they may have had to support the Southern cause, since doing so would now be viewed as engaging in human bondage.

For the many disabled veterans of the war, like Dean, the fear was that the government would create a class of dependent men living "dull and wretched" lives in federal hospitals. However, government planners argued that disabled veterans should be returned to their homes and families, and that they be given the "lighter occupations" in the community - and that they receive a pension.

Beginning in 1861, the U.S. government generously attended to the needs of its soldiers and sailors, or their dependents. Because the federal government did not implement conscription until 1863, these first Civil War benefits in many ways were an attempt to induce men to volunteer. Although altered somewhat over the years, the 1862 statute remained the foundation of the federal pension system until the 1890s. It stipulated that only those soldiers whose disability was "incurred as a direct consequence of . . . Military duty" or developed after combat "from causes which can be directly traced to injuries received or diseases contacted while in military service" could collect pension benefits. The amount of each pension depended upon the veteran's military rank and level of disability. Pensions given to widows, orphans, and other dependents of deceased soldiers were always figured at the rate of total disability according to the military rank of their deceased husband or father. By 1873, widows could also receive extra benefits for each dependent child.

By the year 1900, these pension payments had become the largest single expenditure of the federal government.

1863: On July 20th, Daniel Webster Cole died while serving during the Civil War in New Orleans. He was the grandson of the patriot Deacon Daniel Cole, and the great grandson of the patriot Elisha Cole Jr., the founder of Coles Mills. He was 22 years old, and served in the 176th Regiment, New York Infantry.

On December 3rd, after serving for 2 years and 2 days in the Union Army, 59th NY Infantry Regiment, William Niles Dean was formally discharged. He had suffered serious injuries at the Battle of Antietam in September of

1862, and now was released from duty to continue his long convalescence.

1864: Charles E. Cole, age 17, the son of Ogden and Sarah White Cole, and the great grandson of the patriot Deacon Daniel Cole, died on July 30th while serving in the Union Army and participating in General Sherman's campaign to take the Confederate stronghold in Atlanta, Georgia. His body was returned to his family, and he is buried in the Kelley Cemetery in Carmel.

1865: In this year, an act was passed by the New York State Legislature allowing for New York City's annexation of the water supplies in the town of Kent, and the acquisition of some of the best farmland in Kent, at Boyd's Corners, just southwest of Mt. Nimham. The City wanted the land for the Croton Aqueduct Water Works, and had feuded with Putnam County for years over water rights. Some of this land was owned by Joshua A. Smalley, the son of Zachariah Smalley and the brother of Nathan and Rev. James C. Smalley. The construction of Boyd's Dam and Reservoir would spell the beginning of the end for many of the milling operations in the vicinity. It certainly led to the demise of Coles Mills, which relied upon the flowing Croton River to operate. And once the mills were gone, farming activity in the area would also fall into decline.

John L. Smalley, of the 6th NY Heavy Artillery Regiment, was freed from a Confederate prisoner of war camp at the close of the Civil War.

Local wounded, injured or sick veterans, in addition to William Niles Dean, included:

- Sgt. Isaac W. Parker, shot in the right ankle near the close of the war;
- Private William D. Smalley, shot through the right leg;
- Private John Parker, chronic dysentery.

1866: Mahala Brown Russell, the wife of Morris Russell, the daughter of Stephen Brown, the granddaughter of the patriot Ebenezer Brown, and a lifelong resident of the Mt. Nimham area, passed away on July 2nd at the age of 65. She was laid to rest in the Union (Halstead) Cemetery.

On December 24th, William D. Light (see Illustration 10) wed Mary Jane Russell, the daughter of Silas and Rebecca Lee Russell of Nimham Road. William D. Light was the son of Moseman B. and Sarah Maria Ferris Light, longtime residents along the northeastern base of the mountain. Light was a proud veteran of the Civil War.

Isaac W. Parker (see Illustration 10), the son of John Rhodes Parker and a veteran of the Civil War, married Sarah Jane Light, the daughter of Henry E. and Susan Jane Ferris Light, on December 29th. They would make their home on the Light farm, previously the homestead of Henry Light's uncle, the patriot Samuel Hawkins, at the northern end of Mt. Nimham on what is now known as "Maynard Road."

1867: The 1867 Beers map of Kent (see Illustration 11, published in 1868) confirmed the location of the Isaac Smalley II farm at the location previously owned by Moseman Light. This is where the Gipsy Trail Club administration building stands today. Wright Wixon's farm could be found at the location

Illustration 10: William D. Light (l.) and Sgt. Isaac W. Parker (r.) *(Courtesy of the Kent Historical Society)*

previously owned by his father, John Wixon, on the top of Cole Shears Road. The Darius Ferris farm location was found at the previous James D. Hyatt location on the lower, eastern side of the mountain on Gipsy Trail Road, which is today owned by the Whipple family. Per the map, Howard Tompkins had taken over the farm previously owned by Polly Gifford, just south of Pine Pond on Gipsy Trail Road. He also owned property a little further south on Gipsy Trail Road, on the western side of the road.

Moseman Hyatt, the owner of the farm as shown on the 1854 map which today is used as the NYS Forest Ranger's headquarters just south of Pine Pond, was replaced in this updated map by William A. Northrup. William

Northrup married Elizabeth ("Eliza") A. Hyatt in 1862, and was a descendent of John Northrup, one of the original settlers in Whang Hollow. Eliza Hyatt's father, George L. Hyatt, was a veteran of the War of 1812.

William A. Northrup was a prominent Republican in this area, and served as Town Assessor for 13 years. His farm was comprised of 160 acres, and was described as being in *"a high state of cultivation"* (Beers, 1897). Their son, Ulysses, served as Overseer of the Poor for three years at the County Alms and Poor House Farm on Gipsy Trail Road. Ulysses remained on the Northrup homestead into the mid-1900s.

Theodore Frelinghuysen Cole (1844-1906), the son of Ogden and Sarah Elizabeth White Cole, and the great grandson of the patriot Deacon Daniel Cole, was found on the 1867 map at the Coles Mills site.

Mrs. Elizabeth Tompkins, the widow of Robert and the mother of Howard, was located in the Coles Mills area on the southwestern side of Mt. Nimham.

On the southeastern end of the mountain, the map identified the Milton Niles Dean farm off of Gipsy Trail Road south of the County Farm. The Deans originally owned a farm on the south side of Dean's Pond on Horsepound Road. The Dean Pond location was once the farm of his grandfather, the patriot John Dean.

The remaining farms of Isaac Smalley, Zachariah Smalley, Mrs. Smalley, Stephen Townsend, and Morris Russell were unchanged from the 1854 R.F. O'Connor map.

1868: James Smalley, the son of the patriot Zachariah Smalley and grandson of the patriot and family patriarch James Smalley, passed away on January 7th at the age of 84, and is buried in the Union (Halstead) Cemetery.

1869: Joseph C. and Polly Boyd Haight purchased the old Solomon Hopkins house and mill from his great-grandson, Addison J. Hopkins. The house was located on the southern end of Mt. Nimham, just south of Boyd's Dam, and is acknowledged by a New York State Historical Marker today. The Haights lived in the old house until their new home was completed, and then the old building was eventually demolished (Bicentennial Committee, 57).

William D. Smalley, the son of Rev. James C. and Elizabeth Wright Smalley, died at the age of 25 from wounds originally suffered during the Civil War. He served in Company G of the 150th N.Y. Infantry. He is buried in the Union (Halstead) Cemetery. This branch of the Smalley family lived along Cole Shear's Road, on the western side of the mountain (see Illustration 11).

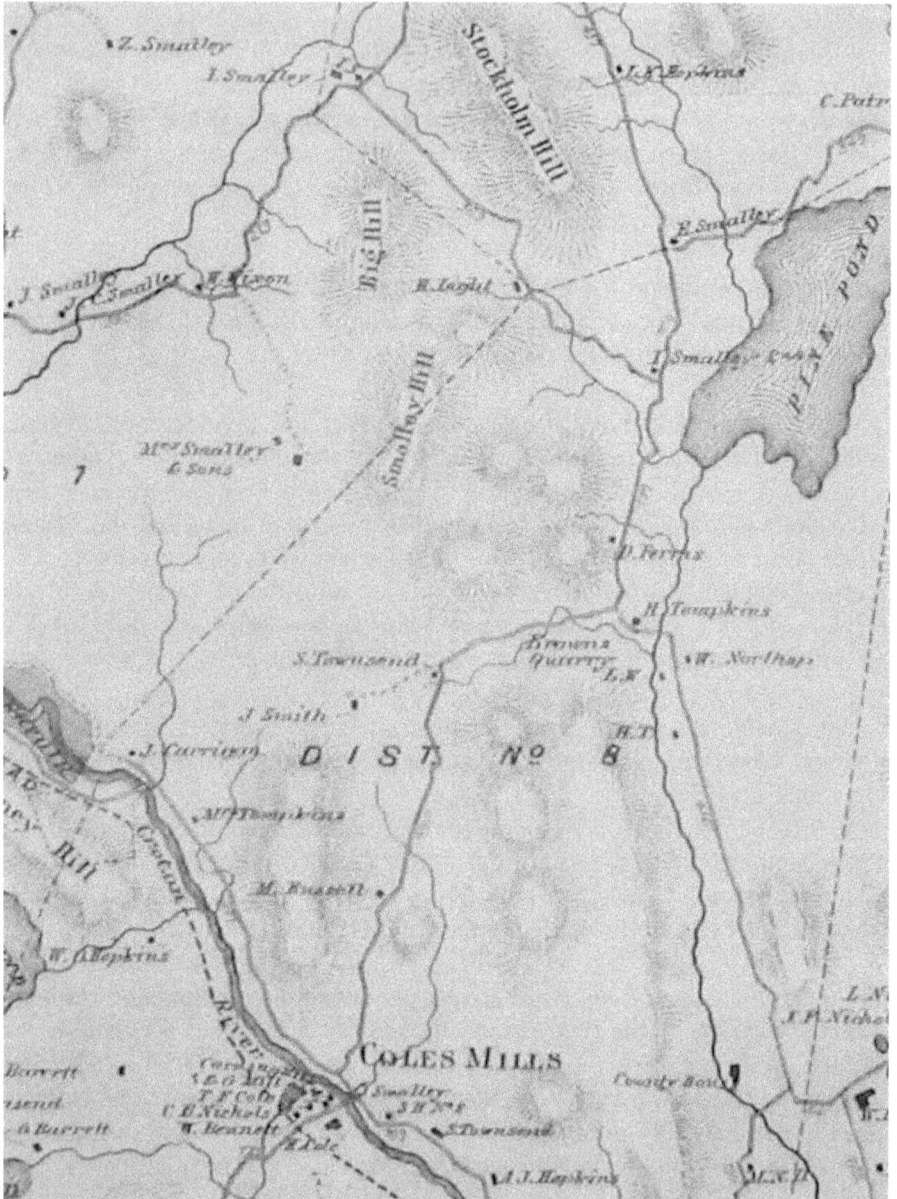

Illustration 11: Excerpt from the 1867 F.W. Beers Map of Kent of the Mt. Nimham Area (published in 1868)

1870: The Federal Census listed the following families and real estate values within the Mt. Nimham area:

- Isaac Smalley: $20,000
- Morris Russell: $3,000
- Darius Ferris: $1,000
- Isaac Smalley II: $2,500
- Henry Light: $4,000
- James C. Smalley: $3,000
- Squire Smalley: $0
- William Northrup: $7,000
- Polly Gifford: $100
- Howard Tompkins: $5,000
- Stephen Townsend: $16,000
- Harmon Cole: $12,000
- Theodore Cole: $6,000
- Elisha Cole: $10,000
- James Smalley: $4,000
- Milton Niles Dean: $6,000

Listed in the census within the Milton Dean household was William Niles Dean, the son who had been severely wounded at the Battle of Antietam. In this census, he was listed as an "invalid" as he was still recovering from the devastating injuries to his face, jaw and spine he had received in September of 1862 at the Battle of Antietam.

1871: Zachariah Smalley, the son of the patriot Zachariah Smalley, husband of Priscilla Odell Smalley, and father of Nathan C. and Rev. James C. Smalley, died on January 14th at the age of 82, and is buried in the Kent and Fishkill Baptist Church Cemetery. His son, the Rev. James C. Smalley, took over the family farm on Cole Shear's Road following the passing of his father.

1874: Morris Russell, a long-time owner of the farm on Coles Mills Road just up the hill from Coles Mills on the southern end of Mt. Nimham, passed away on May 1st at the age of 71, and is buried in the Union (Halstead) Cemetery. His wife, Mahala Brown Russell, predeceased him in 1866.

Morris Russell was the son of the Revolutionary War patriot James Russell, and the nephew of the patriot Lt. Thomas Russell, both of whom were original tenant farmers on Mt. Nimham. Remnants of the Russell family farm can still be found on Coles Mills Road.

On June 12th, Phebe Jane Haviland Dean passed away at the age of 62. She was the wife of Milton Niles Dean, who owned the farm on the southeastern side of Mt. Nimham. She was the mother of John Haviland Dean, who died of measles during the Civil War in 1862, and William Niles Dean, who suffered lifelong injuries during the Battle of Antietam. She was buried in the Raymond Hill Cemetery. She was survived by her husband, sons William and Colonel, and daughter Nancy.

Henry E. Light, the longtime owner of a farm on the northern end of Mt. Nimham, died on July 1st at the age of 66, and is buried in the Union (Halstead) Cemetery. His son-in-law, Isaac W. Parker, then took over the Light farm on the northern side of Mt. Nimham along Maynard Road. It is reported that Henry Light had moved from Kent sometime after 1867, and was living in western New York when he passed away. His body was brought back for burial in his hometown. Isaac Parker was a veteran of the Civil War and was the great-grandson of the patriot Nathaniel Parker.

According to the Putnam County Courier in 1874, *"Theodore Cole of Coles Mills . . . commenced an action against New York City for damages by . . . Boyd's Reservoir . . . Mr. Cole was the owner of four mills situated on the West Branch of the Croton. Prior to the reservoir, Mr. Cole had leased these mills to a Mr. Mallet, who had just recovered a judgment for damages sustained by him for the stoppage of the flow of water from the mills . . . The diversion of the stream from the mills rendered them useless to Mr. Cole, who wanted $10,000 damages"* (Putnam County Historian's Office, as reprinted by Whipple and White, 55).

Mallet was awarded $895 for his losses as a result of the diversion of the water supply by New York City. This became the precedent for the actions by Theodore Cole and others impacted by New York City's watershed activities in this area.

1875: On October 23rd, Asahel Cole, a veteran of the War of 1812, passed away at the age of 89. He was the grandson of the patriot Elisha Cole Jr., who had founded Coles Mills. Asahel is buried in the Kelley Cemetery in Carmel.

1876: Priscilla Odell Smalley, the widow of Zachariah Smalley, died at the age of 92 and is buried in the Kent and Fishkill Baptist Church Cemetery.

The 1876 Thomas Reed Map of Kent (see Illustration 12) identified the J.K. McDaniel farm at the location previously owned by John Wixon (1854 map) and Wright Wixon (1867 map) on Cole Shears Road. Wright Wixon had moved to Horsepound Road along Townsend Ridge, at the old Townsend farm site now known as the "Rockridge Farm."

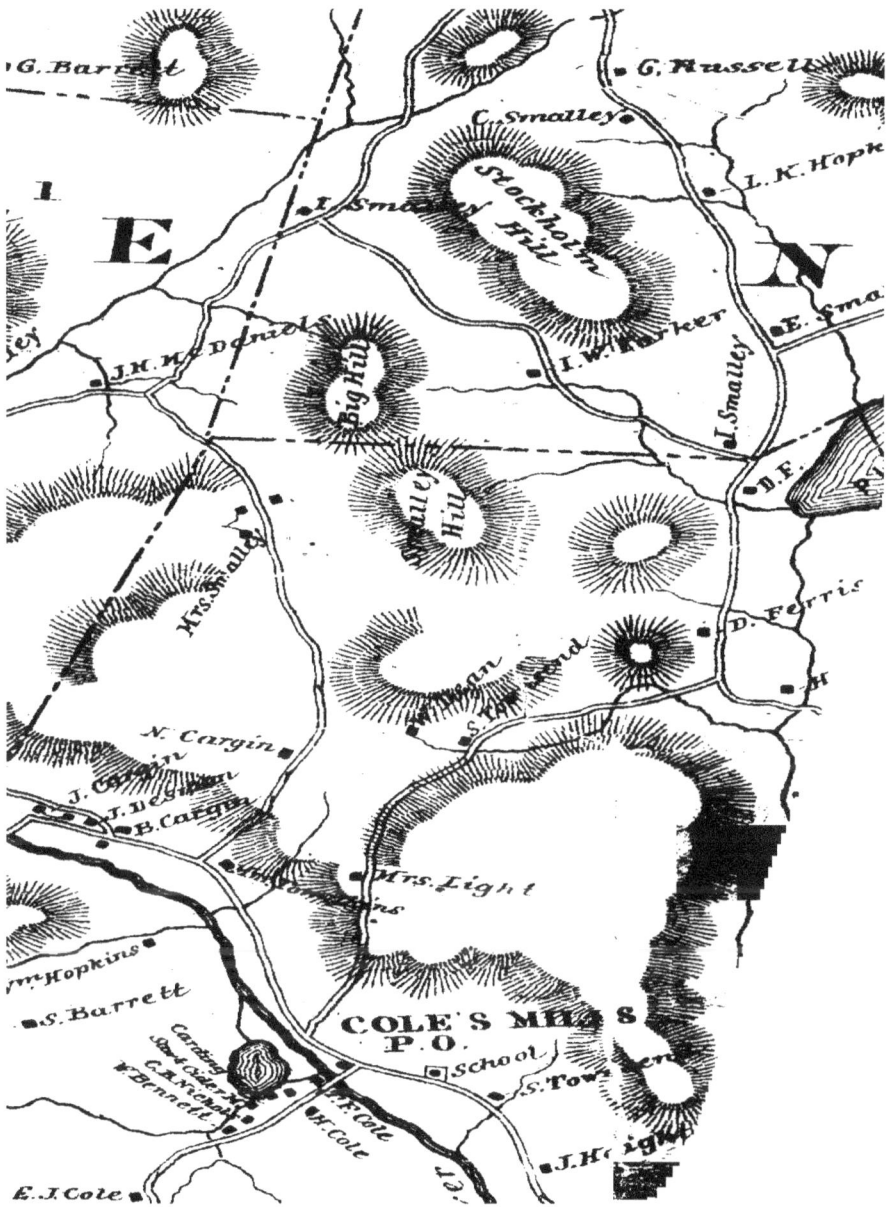

Illustration 12: Mt. Nimham Area Excerpt From the 1876 Thomas Reed Map of Kent (*Courtesy of the Putnam County Historian's Office*)

Isaac W. Parker was found at the previous Henry E. Light location, at the northern end of the mountain. Parker, a Civil War veteran, was Henry's son-in-law. "Mrs. Light" (who is most likely the widow of Henry E. Light, Susan Jane Ferris Light) was identified at the location previously owned by Morris

Russell, who died in 1874, along Coles Mills Road.

The site that was previously owned by Joseph Smith and Stephen Brown (just up the hill from the Stephen Townsend farm) was now listed for "W. Dean" on the 1876 map. This marked another milestone in the remarkable story of William Niles Dean's recovery from the devastation of war. The son of Milton Niles Dean, who owned a farm on Gipsy Trail Road south of Nichols Street (which extended westward to Old Nichols Street and the southeastern portion of Mt. Nimham), William Niles Dean was a veteran of the Civil War, serving in the 59th Infantry Regiment, Company I. He was seriously wounded at Antietam in September of 1862 at the age of 18, losing part of his jaw, making speech difficult, and injuring his back. In the six years since the last census, Dean had recovered sufficiently to follow in his father's footsteps as an outstanding farmer. It is reported in the "Beers Biographical Sketches" that he became an expert fruit farmer following the war. The mountain still shows remaining evidence of this fruit growing past.

Interestingly, Google Maps shows an offshoot of the road leading up to the fire tower labeled as "Uncle WN's Path" (Edward Illiano; Google Maps). This is undoubtedly named for William Niles Dean by his niece and nephew, Florence and Walter Dean, the children of William's younger brother, Colonel Fremont Dean. They had all lived on the mountain in the late 1800s along the road that leads up to the fire tower. "Uncle WN's Path" winds down from near the top of the mountain, down along the western side toward the Smalley Farm, which is now the Clearpool Education Center.

Since Zachariah Smalley's death in 1871, the farm located east of Nimham Road was now shown as "G. Barrett" on the 1876 map. The Coles Mills area no longer included the "J. Smalley Store."

Per the map, the Darius Ferris, Howard Tompkins, and Stephen Townsend farms were still found on the eastern side of Mt. Nimham.

1877: Mary Smalley, the widow of Samuel, and mother of Samuel, Squire, and Coleman, passed away on August 10th at the age of 77. Mrs. Smalley lived on what is now Clearpool Road, on the western side of Mt. Nimham. The maps of the 1800s showed this location as "Mrs. Smalley and Sons." Their classic log cabin/carriage house home with a very large stone fireplace still graces the property north of the Clearpool Education Center.

Mrs. Smalley is buried in the First Baptist Church of Kent Cliffs Cemetery. Her husband had passed away some time before 1845.

1878: Mary "Polly" Smalley Townsend, the wife of Stephen Townsend, the mother of Coleman S. ("Judge Townsend"), and a long-time resident on the Fairview Farm on Mt. Nimham, passed away on December 30th at the age of 67, and is buried in the First Baptist Church of Kent Cliffs Burial Ground. She was the daughter of Isaac and Elizabeth Russell Smalley, and the granddaughter of the patriot Zachariah Smalley.

1879: Stephen Townsend, the grandson of Stephen and the son of Coleman ("Judge Townsend"), was born on January 2nd. Stephen would become a miner and stone mason, and a prolific builder in the town of Kent. He reportedly built the John E. Hayes house, the beautiful stone house on the eastern end of East Boyd's Road. It is reported that Hayes was a famous songwriter of the early 1900s. Townsend also reportedly built the home on Route 301 that would eventually be owned at one time by the actor Edward Hermann. He also reportedly built the stone house adjacent to Boyd's Dam, and was helped in that endeavor by his son, Ken Townsend.

1880: The Federal Census listed the following families living in the Mt. Nimham area:

- Isaac Smalley Jr.
- Alonzo Ferris
- Darius Ferris
- Howard Tompkins
- William A. Northrup
- Milton N. Dean
- Isaac W. Parker
- Isaac Smalley III
- Augustus B. Smalley
- James C. Smalley
- Theodore F. Cole
- Stephen Townsend
- Harmon Cole
- Coleman S. Townsend
- James K. Smalley

This census also confirmed the progress made by William Niles Dean in his recovery from war injuries. As opposed to the 1870 census in which he was listed as an "invalid," the 1880 census listed him as a "farmer." The 1876 map pointed to the area just up the hill from the Fairview Farm as the location of his farm, which was easily accessible to his father's farm on the southeastern base of the mountain. The Deans traveled via Coles Mills Road in shuttling between the two farms.

1883: Harmon Cole, the son of Eleazer and Charity Cole, passed away on March 8th at the age of 69. Harmon Cole owned an extensive farm in Coles Mills, adjacent to the West Branch of the Croton River.

The Town of Kent Assessment Roll for 1883 showed the following farms on Mt. Nimham and their associated acreage:

- William Dean: 125 acres;
- Milton N. Dean: 100 acres;
- Stephen Townsend (3 parcels): 130, 200 & 20 acres;
- Isaac Smalley: 360 acres;
- Howard Tompkins: 180 acres

1886: Isaiah Smalley II died at the age of 101 years and 9 months in this year. He had been raised on the farm of his father, Isaiah, which previously belonged to his grandfather, the patriot James Smalley. In the ensuing years he had owned a farm on North Richardsville (Dicktown) Road. The Brewster Standard recorded the following obituary on April 30th: *"Isaiah Smalley, the centarian of Kent Cliffs, died last Saturday. He was one year and nine months over 100 years. The father of the deceased also lived to be over one hundred years old."*

On February 17th, Colonel Fremont Dean, the son of Milton Niles Dean and the younger brother of William Niles Dean, married Margaret Clark, the daughter of John Clark of Long Island City. Along with their children Florence H. and Walter N. Dean, they would make their home alongside that of his brother William and sister Nancy on Mt. Nimham along what is now the road that leads up to the fire tower. The remains of their home, in the form of stone steps leading up to a rock formation that served as the home's foundation, can still be seen from the roadway (see Illustration 27). This home would have offered wonderful views of Whang Hollow to the east.

1887: Florence Haviland Dean, the niece of William Niles Dean and John Haviland Dean, was born on Lincoln's Birthday, February 12th, 1887. She was the daughter of Colonel Fremont Dean and his wife, Margaret Sarah Clark Dean.

On September 30th, William A. Northrup passed away at the age of 51. He owned the tenant house on Gipsy Trail Road which is now the NYS Ranger's headquarters, in addition to his home which was later destroyed by fire, on the lower eastern base of Mt. Nimham. This property had previously been owned by the Brown family. His son, Ulysses C. Northrup, would continue living on the family farm until the mid-1900s.

It was reported that "Indian Joe Smalley," a Wappinger descendant who hunted and produced charcoal on the mountain throughout this period, also passed away in 1887. He had reportedly served as a scout during the Civil War (Greenwood).

1888: Moseman B. Light passed away on December 8th at the age of 73. Along with his brother, Henry E. Light, Moseman owned property at the northeastern end of Mt. Nimham. He was once the owner of the location where the Gipsy Trail administration building now stands. Moseman was buried in the Kent Cliffs Baptist Church Cemetery, and was survived by his wife, Sarah Maria Ferris Light, and their son, William D. Light.

On August 29th, Addison J. Hopkins, Esquire, a Civil War veteran, passed away at the age of 75. Addison was the grandson of the patriot Jeremiah Hopkins, and great-grandson of the patriot Captain Solomon Hopkins. Addison was a farmer and attorney, and lived on the Hopkins family homestead nearly his entire life. He is buried in the Raymond Hill Cemetery.

1890: In 1890 the most notable revision of the Federal pension law occurred: the Dependent Pension Act. A result of the intense lobbying effort of the veterans' organization, "The Grand Army of the Republic," this statute removed the link between pensions and service-related injuries, allowing any veteran who had served honorably to qualify for a pension if at some time he became disabled and unable to perform manual labor. By 1906 old age alone became sufficient justification for a veteran to receive a pension.

1891: Darius Ferris, the owner of the farm on the lower eastern side of Mt. Nimham on Gipsy Trail Road now known as "Pine View Farm", passed away on March 19th at the age of 78. He is buried in the First Baptist Church of Kent Cliffs Cemetery.

1892: The Town of Kent Assessment Roll for 1892 shows the following farms and acreage on and around Mt. Nimham:

- William Dean: 125 acres;
- Milton N. Dean: 100 acres;
- Stephen Townsend (3 parcels): 130, 200 & 20 acres;
- Coleman R. Shear: 300 acres

1893: Stephen Townsend, the owner of the "Fairview Farm" on the eastern side of Mt. Nimham, and the grandson of the patriot Lt. Col. Elijah Townsend, died on April 26th at the age of 82, and is buried in the Kent Cliffs Baptist Church Burial Ground. Stephen Townsend owned the farm located on the corner of Mt. Nimham Court and Coles Mills Road (now the NYS DEC parking area) for many years throughout the 1800s, and is found at that location on the published maps of 1854, 1867 and 1876. He also owned property down near Coles Mills, just to the east of the Coles Mills Schoolhouse, or Schoolhouse No. 8. His son, Judge Coleman Townsend, continued on the family farm, which included approximately 1,000 sheep, 60 cows, horses, pigs, chickens, several pasture fields and hay fields.

1894: In this year, Isaac Smalley, the son of Isaiah Smalley Jr., passed away at the age of 80. Isaac was a veteran of the Mexican War of 1846-1848. His family had previously owned property on Mt. Nimham following the passing of the patriot James Smalley.

The U.S. Geological Survey Map (see Illustration 13), commissioned by the Department of the Interior in this year, continued to show the farm sites that were once owned by Stephen Townsend, Morris Russell, Howard Tompkins, Darius Ferris, William Northrup, Henry Light/Samuel Hawkins, Isaac Smalley, Zachariah Smalley, Mrs. Smalley, and Milton Dean(e).

This map also included and elevation measurement at the mountain's true peak (next to the fire tower's location): 1,426 feet. The often quoted elevation of 1,244 feet is actually measured on the high ridge known as "Big Hill," which is located at the northern end of Mt. Nimham. This mistake has been often repeated by nearly everyone who has ever quoted the elevation of Mt. Nimham. However, current USGS statistics claim that the elevation at the true peak of the mountain is 1,276 feet. This difference in reported elevation (1,426 versus 1,276) is quite sizeable, and cannot be explained solely due to the difference in measurement instruments used to record the elevation. The reason this issue is significant is due to the fact that if the elevation were 1,426 feet, this would make it the highest point in Putnam County (Mt. Taurus, or Bull Hill, the recognized highest point in Putnam County, is measured at 1,420 feet by the USGS).

At the southern end of the mountain, the map showed the extension of the West Branch Reservoir by New York City. The water covers the area where "Coles Mills" were once located.

1896: On September 25th, Henry Clay Cole, age 55, passed away. He was a veteran of the Civil War, and was the great-grandson of the Revolutionary War patriot Deacon Daniel Cole. He was laid to rest in the Raymond Hill

Cemetery.

The Town of Kent Assessment Roll for 1896 showed the following Mt. Nimham properties:

- William Dean: 125 acres;
- Milton Dean: 73 acres;
- Howard Tompkins: 180 acres;
- Stephen Townsend (3 parcels): 92, 200 & 20 acres

Illustration 13: Excerpt from the 1894 USGS Map of the Mt. Nimham Area (Note the "1426" elevation at the top of the mountain, in the center of this excerpt) (*Courtesy of the United States Interior Department*)

1897: Milton Niles Dean, a longtime farmer on the southeastern side of Mt. Nimham, and the father of Civil War casualties John Haviland Dean and William Niles Dean, passed away at the age of 82. He was survived by his sons William and Colonel, and daughter Nancy. Dean was laid to rest in the Raymond Hill Cemetery alongside his wife, Phebe Jane Haviland Dean, and son, Civil War casualty John Haviland Dean.

1898: Eli Kelley Cole, the great-great-grandson of the patriot Captain Elisha Cole Jr. from the War of Independence, served in the Regular Army and participated in the Spanish American War.

1899: On March 2nd, Howard Tompkins passed away at the age of 71. He was a long-time farmer and resident of the lower eastern side of Mt. Nimham, south of Pine Pond, and adjacent to the Northrup farm. He was laid to rest in the First Baptist Church of Kent Cliffs Cemetery.

Late 1800s: A wooden watch tower was built by the Smalley family on the very top of "Smalley Hill." It was called "Zachariah's Lookout," named after Zachariah Smalley (Kathleen Kane, Interview with Ken and Ella Townsend, 2000). This moniker, and a variation of it known as "Zachary's Lookout," was sometimes applied to the mountain as a whole as a colloquial description by the local residents during this time period.

Late 1800's - Early 1900's: Agriculture and farming began to decline, and lost its place as the major industry of the area around 1930. Milk production, which peaked around 1900, declined significantly after the closing of the Elgin Gilt-edged Butter and Cheese Factory at Farmers Mills in 1907, followed by the closing of the Borden Factory in Brewster in 1917. Also, with New York City obtaining and flooding some of the best farmland in the town near Boyd's Corners and Coles Mills, farm output had significantly dropped as a result. The remaining farmers in this area increasingly turned to fruit and poultry farming.

With the building of the reservoirs by New York City, Coles Mills effectively disappeared under the newly constructed West Branch Reservoir. New York City had widened the West Branch of the Croton River channel, where the mills had been located, to expand the water storage capacity. With the diversion of the water supplies in this area, New York City effectively closed the remaining mills, thus furthering the decline of agriculture in this area. Since agriculture had been the dominant industry, the population fell drastically and precipitously reduced property values throughout the area.

Chapter 6

Mount Nimham in the 20th Century

Having preserved the Union with their blood and supreme sacrifice, the residents of the Mount Nimham area would continue to face great changes and challenges. New York City's annexation and diversion of the local water supplies in the late 1800s had dealt a death blow to the mills, and helped to fuel the further decline in agriculture within this area. But this decline would also help to stimulate the transformation from an agrarian economy to one based on recognizing and capitalizing upon the great natural beauty of the region. The residents of Mount Nimham would also face the scourges of two world wars as the United States took its place as the leader of the free world, and the arsenal of democracy . . .

1900: It was around this time that the "Silver Mine Hole", located near Brown's Quarry on the lower, eastern side of Mt. Nimham, was re-opened by the D. S. Chemical Company. The renewed interest in this mine was sparked by a local mining engineer who determined there was an abundance of arsenical iron pyrites to be found at this location. However, the only smelting forge capable of turning out a truly refined product was located in England, so the mine was eventually closed for good around 1917-1918 (Flato, 70).

The 1900 Federal Census documented the following farms and families on and around Mt. Nimham:

- William Niles Dean, farmer, along with his sister, Nancy L.;
- Coleman Shear, farmer, along with his wife Ellen, and her mother, Elizabeth Smalley, and a boarder named Elvin Mead;
- Isaac W. Parker, farmer, his wife Isabel, and their daughter Eva B.;
- Ulysses Northrup, farmer, his wife Eliza C., and his sister Carrie E.;
- Coleman S. Townsend ("Judge Townsend"), farmer, his wife Rachel, and their sons Coleman S., Hamilton F., and Stephen;
- Daniel H. Cole, farmer, his wife Lottie S., and 'servant' Lewis E. Barrett;
- Joseph Light, stone mason, his wife Phebe, their son George, and daughter Annie;
- Harrison Ferris, farm laborer, his wife Charlena, their daughters Bertha and Anna B., and sons William and George.

1901: The Clearpool Education Center, located on the western slope of Mt. Nimham, was founded in this year as a summer camp. The purpose of the

Center was to offer disadvantaged children from New York City a temporary escape from inner city life. The Clearpool Education Center is located on the farm previously owned by Samuel and Mary Smalley and their sons, Samuel, Squire and Coleman Smalley.

1903: The Reverend James C. Smalley, the son of Zachariah Smalley and a long-time owner of a farm on the western side of Mt. Nimham, passed away on June 11th at the age of 79, and was laid to rest in the Union (Halstead) Cemetery. Rev. Smalley served the faithful in the First Baptist Church of Kent Cliffs from 1852 to 1869, and then at the Kent and Fishkill Baptist Church until 1877. He also preached for a time at the Second Kent Baptist Church. He was the grandson of the patriot Zachariah Smalley.

1906: Stephen Kenneth Townsend (Ken) was born on February 25th, the son of Stephen and Anna Augusta Light Townsend, she being the granddaughter of Moseman Light. Ken Townsend was the grandson of Judge Coleman S. Townsend, and the great-great-great-grandson of the patriot Lt. Col. Elijah Townsend.

On June 14th, the Bronx Chapter of the Daughters of the American Revolution dedicated a large cairn and plaque in Van Cortlandt Park to honor the sacrifice of the patriot Chief Daniel Nimham and his brave brothers, who made the supreme sacrifice for our liberty on August 31, 1778 (Illustration 14). Made from fieldstone conglomerate, with a bronze plaque cast by the Henry – Bonnard Bronze Company, the monument measures a height of 6'6", with a width and depth of 4' each.

The monument's inscription reads:

"AUGUST 31, 1778
UPON THIS FIELD, CHIEF NIMHAM AND SEVENTEEN
STOCKBRIDGE INDIANS AS ALLIES OF THE PATRIOTS,
GAVE THEIR LIVES FOR LIBERTY.
ERECTED BY THE BRONX CHAPTER, DAUGHTERS OF THE
AMERICAN REVOLUTION
MOUNT VERNON, NEW YORK.
JUNE 14, 1906"

Theodore Frelinghuysen Cole, age 62, passed away on December 6th and was laid to rest in the Kelley Cemetery. He was the great-grandson of the patriot Deacon Daniel Cole, and was the last of the millers at Coles Mills, before the annexation of the local water sources by New York City and subsequent re-routing of the water supply spelled the end of the mills in

Illustration 14: Chief Nimham Memorial in Van Cortlandt Park *(Photo courtesy of the Nimham Mountain Singers)*

the town of Kent.

1907: The Elgin Gilt-Edged Butter and Cheese Factory at Farmers Mills, finding it impossible to compete with newer factories located near the rail lines, was dissolved in April. This effectively signaled the end of Farmers Mills as a thriving community. It also limited the local farmers in terms of future dairy farming opportunities in this area. Gradually over time, the remaining farmers focused on apple and poultry farming.

1909: On October 27th, Addison Reed Hopkins (1884-1971) married Florence Haviland Dean (b. 1887). Addison was the grandson of Civil War veteran Addison J. Hopkins, Esquire, who was the grandson of the Revolutionary War patriot Jeremiah Hopkins, and the great-grandson of the Revolutionary patriot Captain Solomon Hopkins. Florence was the daughter of Colonel Fremont Dean, the younger brother of Civil War veterans John Haviland and William Niles Dean, and she was the great-great-granddaughter of the Revolutionary War patriot John Dean. The Hopkins family were longtime residents of the southeastern base of Mt. Nimham, along the Philipstown Turnpike (which is now Route 301), dating to pre-Revolution times.

1910: With many local farmers ready to sell their land, a few wealthy New York City businessmen purchased approximately 900 acres between the northern end of Mt. Nimham and the middle of Whang Hollow, for use in hunting, fishing and other recreational uses. Fancying themselves as outdoor adventurers, they turned to the poetic adventure writer of their era, Rudyard Kipling, for inspiration. Kipling had previously published a poem in 1892 entitled "The Gipsy Trail," which reportedly would become the namesake for the twisty, narrow, bouncy road that now bears this name (see Appendix F).

When their interest eventually lagged, developer Carl Anderson organized the Gipsy Trail Camp and Country Club, and built a log clubhouse overlooking Pine Pond in 1925. In 1956, the original clubhouse was destroyed by fire, and was replaced by the current structure on the same site. The current site of the administration building, located at the corner of Gipsy Trail and Maynard Road, is the same location where Moseman Light, and later Isaac Smalley Jr., had lived for many years throughout the 1800s.

Over the years, additional land was purchased, helping to preserve the northern end of Mt. Nimham and western portion of Whang Hollow to this day. Whang Hollow Road, accessible from Gipsy Trail Road northeast of the club's administration building, was divided into two sections, with the northern section now being known as "Whangtown Road."

The 1910 Federal Census listed the following families and farms on and around Mt. Nimham:

- Coleman Shear, farmer, and his wife, Ellen Smalley Shear (she being the daughter of Isaac and Esther Smalley);
- Isaac W. Parker, farmer, and his wife, Isabel Smalley Parker;
- William N. Dean, farmer, his sister Nancy L., and 'servant' Vincent Barrett;
- Ulysses Northrup, farmer, his sister Carrie E., and farm laborer Silas Smith, and his sister Rebecca;
- Coleman S. Townsend ("Judge Townsend"), farmer, his wife Rachel, and sons Coleman and Hamilton F.;
- Alonzo Ferris, farmer, son Edward, daughter Anna E. Robinson, and son-in-law William Robinson;
- Stephen Townsend, miner, his wife Anna, sons Clarence J. and Stephen K. (Ken), and daughter Velma.

Stephen Townsend, who is listed in the census as a "miner," is believed to be the individual who built the explosives bunker on the Fairview Farm, which can be found today adjacent to the DEC parking area on the mountain.

1911: William D. Smalley, a veteran of the Civil War (Company G, 6th NY Heavy Artillery Regiment), and the grandson of the patriot Isaiah Smalley, died at the age of 83 on July 11th, and is buried in the Russell-Mead Cemetery. He had survived two wives, Thankful Jane Ressique and Lucinda Merritt, and was survived by his then current wife, Sarah Jane Worden.

1912: Albert B. Hines became the Executive Director of the Madison Square Boys Club in Manhattan. Under his guidance, Camp Albert B. Hines would be established on the northwestern side of Mt. Nimham, just north of Clearpool Camp, with which it was affiliated. Camp Hines would specialize in providing an alternative for teenage boys who would otherwise be induced to join destructive gangs in the city. Some of the older boys helped to build the open-faced lean-to cabins, which accommodated ten boys each. A small lake and pond were created to provide a cool retreat from the steamy city streets (Madison Square Boys and Girls Club).

1913: Isaac W. Parker passed away on February 4th, just one week short of his 71st birthday. He lived on the farm previously owned by his father-in-law, Henry Light, and by the patriot Samuel Hawkins previous to that, on the northern side of Mt. Nimham along what is now called Maynard Road (named after Harry Maynard). Isaac Parker was a veteran of the Civil War, having served as a sergeant in the 6th NY Heavy Artillery Regiment, Co. G. He came from a long line of distinguished war veterans from this family dating back to the Revolution. Isaac Parker was laid to rest in the Smalley Burial Ground.

1914: On April 8th, William Niles Dean passed away at the age of 70. He was a veteran of the Civil War, serving in the 59th Infantry Regiment, Company I. Dean had been seriously wounded at the Battle of Antietam in September of 1862, having lost part of his jaw, making speech difficult, and injuring his back. He later became a very successful fruit farmer while living on the upper eastern side of Mt. Nimham, just above Stephen and Coleman Townsend's "Fairview Farm," at the site which was previously owned by Stephen Brown and James Smith. Dean's family also owned the farm on Gipsy Trail Road, south of Nichols Street, which extended up the southeastern side of the mountain. He never married, most likely due to his extensive injuries suffered during the war. His sister, Nancy Letitia Dean, cared for him throughout his life following the war, and she never married as well. William Niles Dean was laid to rest in the Raymond Hill Cemetery, alongside his parents and brother, John Haviland Dean, who died from measles during the Civil War in January of 1862. He was survived by his sister and younger brother, Colonel Fremont Dean, who continued to live and work on the Mt. Nimham farm.

1915: Coleman S. Townsend, the son of Stephen and Mary Polly Smalley Townsend, and known popularly as "Judge Townsend" for his many years of service as Justice of the Peace, died at the age of 64. He was laid to rest in the First Baptist Church of Kent Cliffs Burial Ground. A longtime farmer on Mt. Nimham, where the DEC parking area is located today, his obituary recalled that *"the farm on which he lived is without doubt the most sightly in Putnam County, as a most unusual view can be had from it many miles in all directions"* (Putnam County Courier).

1916-1918: The following individuals associated with Mt. Nimham served their country during the First World War:

- Eli Kelley Cole, the great-great grandson of the patriot Captain Elisha Cole, Jr. and a veteran of the Spanish American War, served in the Regular Army and participated in the First World War. He eventually reached the rank of Major General;
- George Tillot Cole, the son of George R. and Mary Ganun Cole, and the great-great-grandson of the patriot Deacon Daniel Cole, also served during the war in the U.S. Navy;
- Thomas Manning Townsend, the son of Byron and Elnora Barrett Townsend, and the great-great-great grandson of the patriot Lt. Col. Elijah Townsend, served as a private in the U.S. Army;
- Robert Stanton Feeley, who served as a sergeant in the 311th Infantry, and later made his home on the Pine View Farm on Gipsy Trail Road at the eastern base of the mountain.

1917-1918: The "Silver Mine Hole", located on the lower eastern side of Mt. Nimham and rich in arsenical ore, was finally closed by the D.S. Chemical Company when it was deemed that there was no nearby smelting forge capable of turning out a satisfactory end product (Flato, 70). Stephen Townsend, the descendant of the original owner of the Fairview Farm located just up the mountain, was reportedly the manager of the mine during this period of time. The mine included two steam engines, one to bring buckets filled with rock out of the mine, and the other to crush the rock. A blacksmith shop was also on site to keep the drills sharpened (Whipple and White, 144).

1918: On November 6th, 1918, George Tillot Cole passed away in a Navy hospital on Gibraltar. He was 23 years old. The cause of death was pneumonia. He was the son of George Richardson and Mary Ganung Cole, and was the great-great grandson of the patriot Deacon Daniel Cole.

1920: The Federal Census lists the following families and farms on and around Mt. Nimham:

"Shears Road":

- Hamilton F. Townsend (age 44), farmer and enumerator of the census;
- Hamilton A. Smalley (78), farmer, his wife Adaline (68), and their daughter Rita Tilford (41);
- George L. Marsh (55), apartment house superintendent, his wife Elizabeth (51), and their son Edgar L. (14);
- Coleman R. Shear (66), farmer, his wife Ellen (66), cousin Parmer Sprague (50), Catherine Townsend (74), and servant Hashagen Rudolph, Jr. (26);
- Edwin D. Brown (43), farmer, his wife Ethel (29), their son Charles E. (10), and daughter Catherine C. (6);

"County Farm Highway":

- Silas L. Russell (55), farmer;
- Edward Ferris (47), laborer, highway department;
- Charles Cartwright (58), laborer, arsenic mine;
- Ulysses Northrup (55), dairy farmer;

"County Poor Farm":

- Russell B. Wixson (60), overseer, and his sister Cynthia (50);

"Smokey Hollow Road":

- Briggs Tompkins (37), laborer, his wife Bertha (35), and daughters Edna M. (7), Minna M. (5), Cassie G. (3), and Blanche B. (1);
- Stephen Townsend (40), farmer, his wife Anna A. (40), sons Clarence J. (18) and Stephen K. (Ken) (13), and daughters Velma A. (10), Grace E. (3), and Dortha L. (10 months);
- Byron E. Townsend (58), laborer, his mother Emaline B. (88), sons Dewit B. (23) and Thomas M. (21), and daughter Zillah L. (19);
- Asbury C. Townsend (60), retired, and his wife Catherine (60);

"Kent Cliffs":

- Daniel H. Cole (51), laborer, his wife Lottie S. (46), son Paul (13) and mother-in-law Matilda Foshay (77);
- Albert G. Cole (55), farmer, his wife Euphemia A. (54), daughter Mildred (12), and boarder Ralph Hewitt (25);

"Kent Cliffs Highway":

- Coleman S. Townsend (45), NYC Watershed Inspector, his wife Flora M. (42), and mother-in-law Sarah J. Williams (84).

As of 1920, Colonel Fremont Dean was no longer listed in the Kent census. However, he was found in the Brooklyn census, along with his wife, Margaret, and son Walter, age 31. Enumerated on January 14th, Colonel was listed as "retired," while Walter's occupation was listed as "accountant". Colonel's wife, Margaret Sarah Clark Dean, was originally from the Long Island City area.

Edwin D. Brown from "Shear's Road" was the great-great grandson of the patriot Ebenezer Brown, who was originally from Gipsy Trail Road across from the mountain.

Early 1920s: According to the late Ken Townsend, the great-grandson of Stephen and Polly Smalley Townsend of the Fairview Farm on Mt. Nimham, he, his father and brother Clarence built a wooden fire tower out of chestnut poles, approximately 60 feet high, to replace the tower previously built by the Smalleys on the top of Mt. Nimham. The original tower built by the Smalleys had been dubbed "Zachariah's Lookout" in honor of Zachariah Smalley (Katherine Kane, Interview with Ken and Ella Townsend). Some local residents came to use this term to describe the mountain itself.

Ken Townsend also recounted that one of the few remaining descendents of the Wappinger, a man known as "Indian Hen Barrett," was an occasional visitor to Mt. Nimham and the remaining Nochpeem forts located on the mountain. According to Townsend, Barrett lived near Long Pond in Carmel, and would drive up the mountain in a horse and wagon, staying for several days at a time (Kane). He reportedly passed away there during one visit.

According to local residents, the mountain, with its rugged terrain and multiple springs and other water sources, became an ideal location for the production of alcohol during Prohibition. Reportedly, there were several stills set up near these springs.

The Town of Kent Highway Department placed a rock crusher on the level land on the corner of Gipsy Trail Road and Mt. Nimham Court, where the first house on the road is located today. They would transport large rocks and boulders from the mountain, crush them, and use the crushed stone for use in building and maintaining the roads in the town. The rock crusher was powered by a World War I - era tank tractor, with bullet holes and all. The foreman in charge of the crusher was Ralph Merritt's father.

1925: The New York State Census listed the following residents of "Coles Mills Hill Road":

- Walter J. Heady
- Briggs D. Tompkins
- Najarro Menendy (Menendez)

"Clear Pond Camp Road":

- Stephen Townsend

1926: William D. Light, a Civil War veteran who grew up living along the northeastern side of the mountain, passed away on January 5th at the age of 83. He was the son of Moseman B. and Sarah Maria Ferris Light, and served in the 6th Heavy Artillery Regiment, Company G, during the war. He eventually owned a dairy farm on Fair Street in Carmel, which was later sold to Borden's Condensery. He had married Mary Jane Russell on December 24, 1866, who survived him. Light was interred in Raymond Hill Cemetery.

1928: The U.S. Geological Survey map of this area (see Illustration 15), produced by the Department of the Interior, continued to show the farm sites previously owned by the Townsend, Russell, Tompkins, Ferris, Smalley, Parker, and Northrup families. It also measured the elevation at the true peak of the mountain as 1,426 feet, consistent with the 1894 USGS map. However, current USGS data suggests the elevation at this point is 1,276 feet above sea level.

New York State formed the "State Reforestation Commission" in 1928 to study the impact of farm abandonment and clear-cutting of the remaining private forestland in the State. This grew out of concern that private land was being reforested at a very slow rate, as compared to the reforestation rate of public lands.

Colonel Fremont Dean, the younger brother of William Niles Dean, died in this year at the age of 72. Colonel Dean had continued on the farm on Mt.

Nimham following the death of his brother in 1914, but had moved to Brooklyn sometime around 1920. He was laid to rest in the Raymond Hill Cemetery along with his parents and brothers, who had predeceased him.

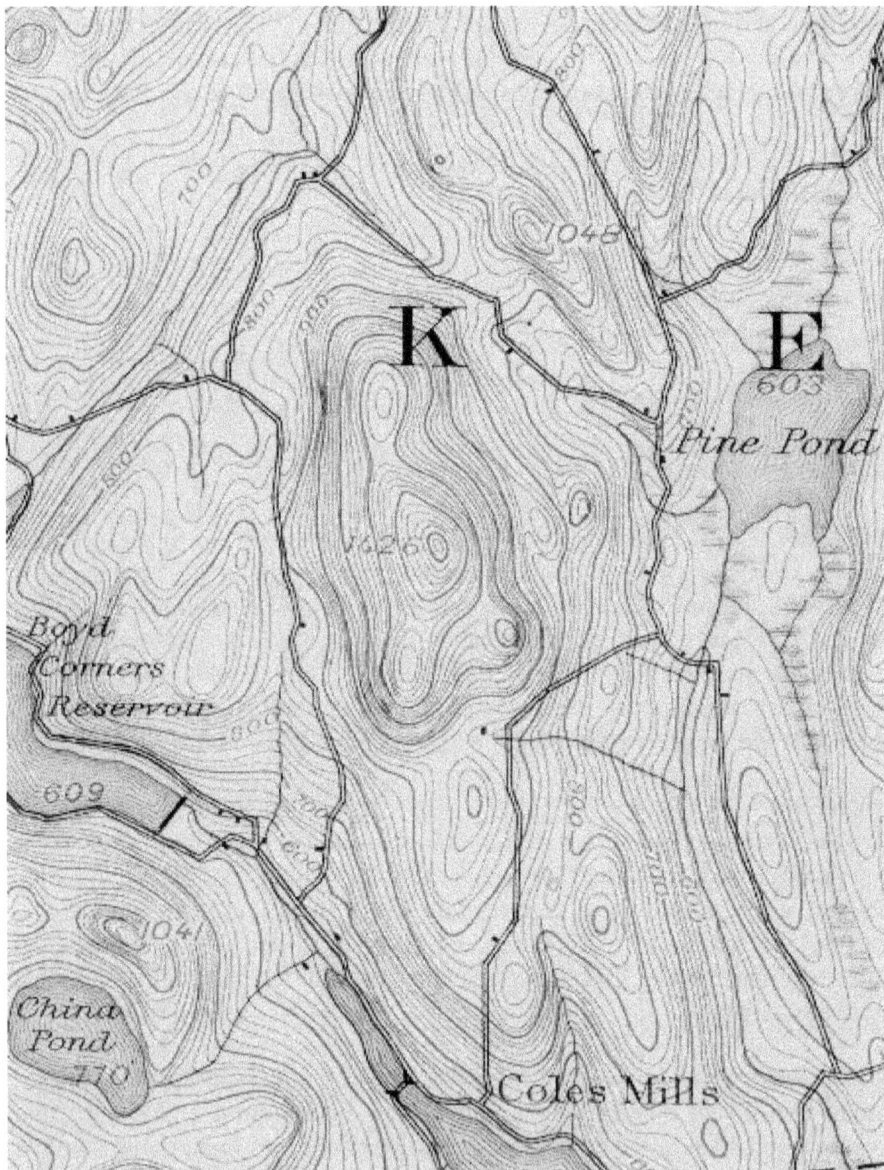

Illustration 15: 1928 USGS Map Excerpt of Mt. Nimham (*Courtesy of the United States Interior Department*)

1929: On May 5th, Nancy Letitia Dean, the younger sister of William Niles Dean and elder sister of Colonel Dean, passed away at the age of 77. She had served as an unfailing caretaker for her brother, the Civil War veteran William Niles Dean, who had suffered life-altering injuries at the Battle of Antietam in 1862, which followed him through the remainder of his life until his death in 1914. She never married, and is buried in the Raymond Hill Cemetery along with her parents and brothers.

On July 4th, Major General Eli Kelley Cole passed away at the age of 61, and was laid to rest in Raymond Hill Cemetery. He was the great-great grandson of Captain Elisha Cole Jr., a patriot of the War of Independence, and the founder of Coles Mills. Major General Cole was a veteran of both the Spanish American War and the First World War.

Based upon recommendations from the State Reforestation Commission, the New York State Legislature passed the "State Reforestation Act" to initiate a program of acquiring and reforesting abandoned farmland. The main objective of the law and its amendments was to retire farmland from agricultural use permanently, and reforest these regions, providing a wide range of resources from timber to public recreational areas. The program mainly attempted to acquire lands that were at least 50% cleared, and suitable for reforestation. The initial planting of new land began in the fall of 1929 in Otsego, Chenango and Cortland counties. These purchases were enabled by the issuance of environmental bond acts and other means authorized by the New York Legislature. The State also pursued a policy of replanting trees in depleted areas.

1930s: During this time period, the Townsends' Fairview Farm was rented to various local residents, including Percy Adams and his family. Percy Adams Jr. would later serve our country in the Second World War. Percy Adams Sr.'s nephew, Adelbert "Snookie" Adams, was a frequent visitor during these years, and remembered the house as being a brown shingled, two-story home with several rooms and a big woodstove. It was located adjacent to the pond, which is next to the DEC parking area. Snookie remembered that there were many apple trees on the mountain, which was also plentiful with deer and grouse. His uncle would hang the deer inside the explosives bunker located nearby the house. He also remembered there being at least one, and possibly two, automobiles parked inside the "garage," which was originally the barn for the Fairview Farm.

Snookie's elder brother and sister attended the one-room Coles Mills Schoolhouse (Schoolhouse No. 8), as they lived on Belden Road.

Local resident Ralph Merritt, who is the brother-in-law of Percy Adams Jr., remembered that they used to hang and smoke pork inside the explosives bunker adjacent to the farm. On the hill above the bunker there was a chicken coop used by the tenants, and previously used by the Townsend family.

On the farm previously owned by James D. Hyatt and later by Darius Ferris on the eastern side of the mountain, the artist Robert Stanton Feeley established "Pine View Farm." The property included the circa 1788 house that sits on the mountainside overlooking the farm. The farmhouse on the eastern side of Gipsy Trail Road was built by Paul Nault. Feeley used the red barn as his studio. He was the creative director of Avon Products and president of Robert S. Feeley Associates, a New York advertising agency (Whipple and White, 140-143).

1930: The Federal Census listed the following families and farms on and around Mt. Nimham:

"Coles Mills - Kent Cliffs Road":

- Briggs Tompkins (47), laborer, his wife Bertha M. (35), their daughters Edna M. (17), Minnie M. (15), Cassie C. (14), and Blanche B. (11), and their sons Charles B. (9), Briggs Jr. (7), Melvin G. (6) and Dan B. (2);
- Nazario Menendez (61), farmer, his wife Fannie R. (65), sister-in-law Eliza Smith (74), and boarder Bertha Gable (7);
- Harry S. Davis (28), laborer, his wife Grace E. (28), and their daughter Mary Etta (1);
- Carl N. Baker (28), mechanic, his wife Lena M. (31), stepdaughter Dorothy Post (9), and daughter Carol I. (2);
- Ernest R. Scott (29), laborer, and his wife Elizabeth M. (32);
- Walter J. Heady (59), farmer, his wife Sarah E. (64), and their grandson Frances (14);
- Stephen Townsend (51), carpenter, his wife Anna A. (51), and their sons Clarence J. (28), S. Kenneth (23), and daughters Velma (20), Grace E. (14), and Dorothy L. (11);

"Gipsy Trail Road":

- Edwin L. Ferris (52), laborer;
- Thomas Barrett (74), laborer, and his brother Harmon (65);
- William D. Robinson (55), farmer, his wife Anna E. (48), and boarder Hamilton Townsend (55), who was listed as "Superintendent - Public Works";
- Ulysses Northrup (64), farmer, and his sister Carrie E. (58);
- Milton I. Ross (31), contractor/builder, his wife Mildred C. (29), their

son Elmer E. (4), and their daughters Jean E. (3) and Dorothy I. (1);

- Antonio Bellenger (27), laborer, his wife Angeline M. (24), and their son Robert A. (3);
- John Burnley (64), tobacco stripper.

"County Farm":

- Eliza W. Dean (45), Public Works Commissioner/County Home, her husband (name illegible) (56), daughter Nina D. (12), and servant Edith Bennett (50).

1933: A 1933 aerial photograph of the Mt. Nimham area (Illustration 16) shows Pine Pond in the upper right side of the photo. The Fairview Farm can be found diagonally down to the left of the southwestern tip of Pine Pond in the lower one-third area of the photo, off of Mt. Nimham Court, and east of Clearpool. The old Isaac Smalley farm can be seen in the upper left corner of the photo.

1938: The New York State Reforestation Act was expanded in 1938 to include properties outside of the Adirondack and Catskill Parks. It was during this time period that portions of Mt. Nimham began to be acquired by the State under this program. Part of the purchase eventually included the Northrup farm on the eastern side of Gipsy Trail Road, across from the mountain. The old Northrup tenant house was eventually used as the NYS DEC Forest Ranger's headquarters, continuing to this day.

1940: Numerous devastating fires, destroying millions of acres of forestland in New York, spurred the creation of fire districts in the early 1900s. Fire towers were erected on mountains within these districts from which spotters could quickly locate potentially dangerous fires caused by sparking locomotives, lightning strikes, careless hunters, or residents burning brush. The CCC (Civilian Conservation Corps), a public works program created during the Depression, was assigned the job of building an improved roadway up to the very top of Mt. Nimham. The fire tower, a 90-foot steel Aermotor tower with a 7' by 7' metal cabin at the top, was put in place by New York State and the CCC, with seasonal fire-watchers assigned to report on any observable fires over the vast countryside visible from the top of Mt. Nimham. Dick Ketchum, who grew up in the Ludingtonville and White Pond areas, was the first fire warden assigned to the tower. A log cabin on top of the mountain, near the fire tower, was used to house the fire watchers. In its first year of operation in 1941, 73 fires and 266 visitors were logged. Mr. Ketchum also served as a local gunsmith, as well as a tattoo artist.

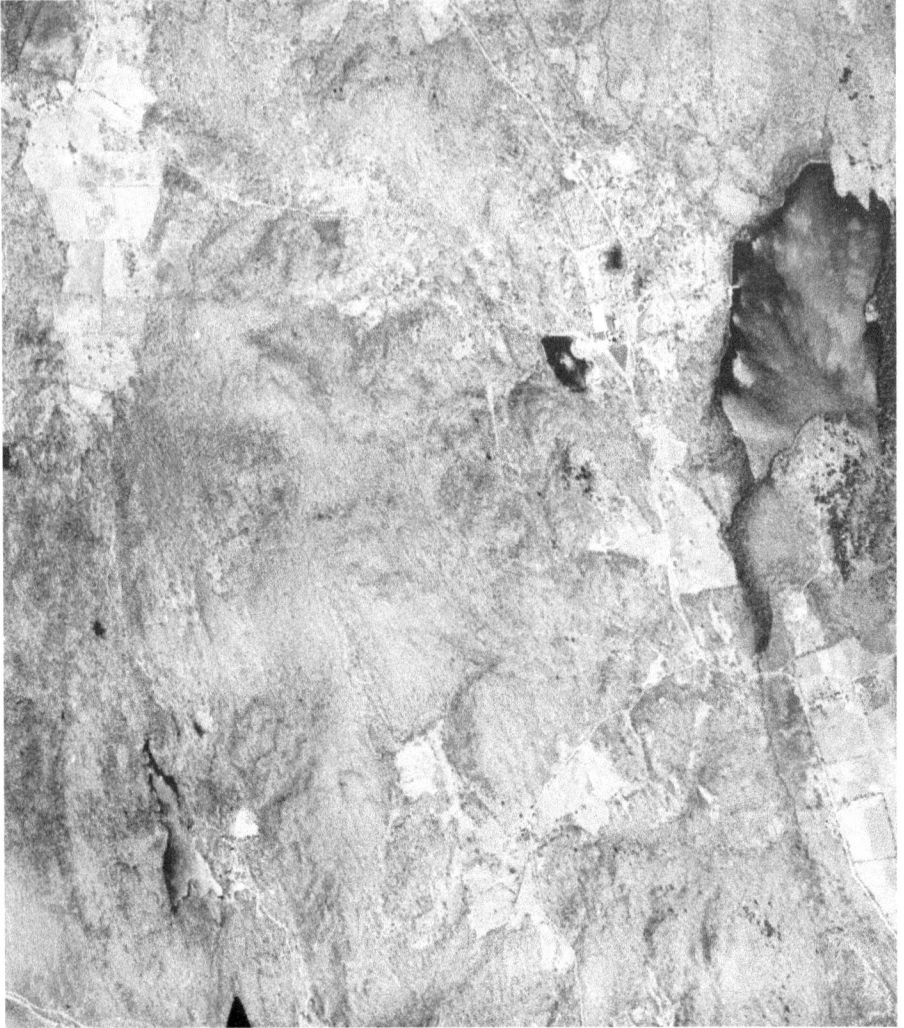

Illustration 16: 1933 Aerial Photo of the Mt. Nimham Area, with Pine Pond shown in the upper right *(Courtesy of the Putnam County Historian's Office)*

During construction of the roadway to the top of the mountain, the CCC, under the guidance of New York State, encountered the remains of the Nochpeem forts that were still standing, nearly 200 years after the Nochpeem and the rest of the Wappinger tribes were removed from their ancestral homeland, and well over 200 years from their original construction. Built with a foundation base of about four feet of stone with another four feet of logs on top, these invaluable artifacts were bulldozed into piles of rubble (Interview with Ken and Ella Townsend, 2000, conducted by Katherine Kane). This blatant disregard for preserving invaluable historic artifacts has

110

led many to criticize the State's stewardship of the mountain over the years.

1941-1945: Following are some of the residents of the Mt. Nimham area who served our country during World War II:

- Stephen Wood ("Woody") Cornell;
- Stephen Kenneth ("Ken") Townsend;
- Ward Cole, the son of Charles P. and Estella Cole;
- Andrew Heady (who was married to Stephen Townsend's daughter, Grace Elizabeth) served as a private in the U.S. Army;
- Percy Adams, Jr.;
- George C. Whipple, Jr.;
- Elmer E. Ross;
- Briggs Tompkins;
- Charles A. Tompkins;
- Leon B. Tompkins, who served as a sergeant in the U.S. Army;
- Melvin G. Tompkins

1943: Two Townsend brothers who grew up on the mountain were elected to public office in the Town of Kent in 1943. Coleman S. Townsend was elected Town Assessor, while his brother, Hamilton Fish Townsend, was elected Superintendent of Highways. Both ran on the Democratic line, while Hamilton also gained the Republican endorsement as well.

1944: The U.S. Geological Survey Map, produced by the Interior Department in 1944, still showed the moniker of "Smalley Mountain" on its map of this area, even though the name had been changed in the late 1800s (see Illustration 17). It also listed an elevation of 1,244 feet at what was known as "Big Hill" on the maps of the 1800s, which is actually the northern-most high ridge on Mt. Nimham. The USGS maps published in 1894 and 1928 pinpointed the true peak of the mountain, and labeled it as being 1,426 feet above sea level. However, the current data sheet from the USGS indicates an elevation of 1,276 feet at this point, which is now being tested thanks to the availability of hand-held GPS devices. This significant discrepancy of 150 feet has never been adequately explained by the USGS.

To the west of the mountain, a new lake appeared on the map: the man-made Clear Pool Lake. And to the north of Clear Pool, another man-made lake, which was part of Camp Albert B. Hines, also appeared for the first time. Camp Hines was affiliated with the Clearpool Camp, but was specifically dedicated to serving teen-age boys from New York City in order to give them an alternative to joining destructive gangs. Remnants of the camp's infrastructure, some of which was built by the campers themselves,

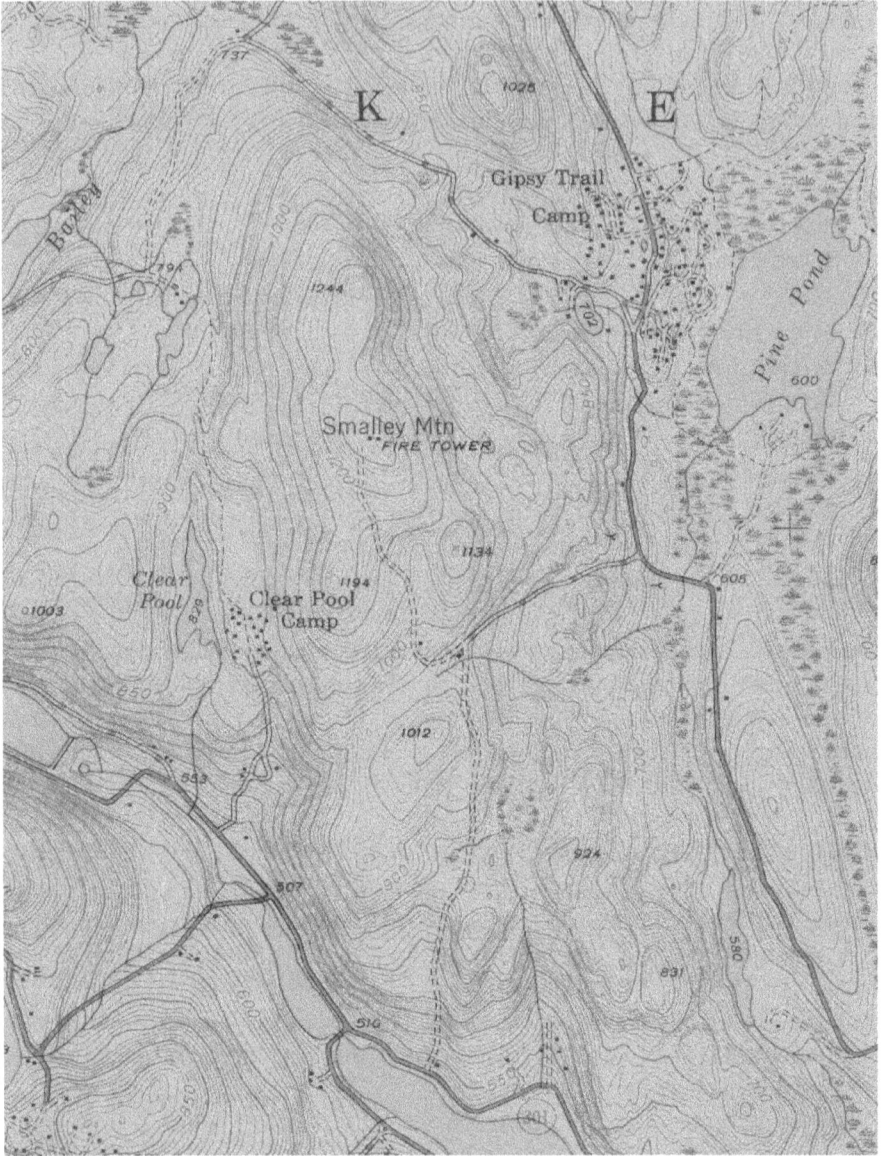

Illustration 17: 1944 USGS Map Excerpt of the Mt. Nimham Area *(Courtesy of the U.S. Interior Department)*

can still be found within the encroaching forest.

The former residence of William Niles Dean was also shown further up the access road leading to the top of the mountain. Today, one can see the steps that led up to the house, which had a magnificent view of Whang Hollow and its eastern border, including Townsend Ridge, Barrett Hill, Beaver Hill, and

Hemlock Ledge (see Illustration 25).

1948: Hamilton Fish Townsend, the son of Judge Coleman S. Townsend and the great-great grandson of the patriot Lt. Col. Elijah Townsend, passed away on August 24th. He was 72 years old, and was laid to rest in the First Baptist Church of Kent Cliffs Cemetery, which had been relocated from Boyd's Reservoir to the hillside above the reservoir. Hamilton Fish Townsend had carried on as a farmer on his family's "Fairview Farm" on Mt. Nimham following his father's death, and had also served as a census enumerator and Highway Superintendent. In his later years he lived on Gipsy Trail Road across from the Pine View Farm.

1950s: A small ski slope was built on the eastern face of Mt. Nimham by Stephen Wood ("Woody") Cornell, owner of the Carmel Lumber Yard and a World War II veteran. Located just north of Mt. Nimham Court, the small slope was serviced by a J-bar and was illuminated for nighttime skiing. The remains of the equipment shed, which housed the power equipment for the tow-bar and lights, are still visible from Gipsy Trail Road (see Illustration 18). Mr. Cornell built a beautiful A-frame chalet nearby for his family's use and easy access to the slope (Rickert-Shatz Family; Ralph Merritt).

Woody Cornell also acknowledged, and celebrated, the existence of the arsenic mine that was once located on his property, which was originally known as "Brown's Silver Mine Hole." He helped create a logo for the signage of the mine, and for his own personal stationery (see Illustration 19). The mine was about 90-feet deep, and was filled with water by this time. Woody Cornell would scuba dive in the frigid water, before hiring local resident Ralph Merritt to fill it in due to safety concerns. It took five days of earth moving and filling to finally complete the job, as Mr. Merritt worked precariously close to the edge of the mine.

In an ironic twist, Mr. Cornell was a direct descendant of Captain John Underhill, the English mercenary hired by Governor Kieft in 1643 to exterminate the local Native population. Underhill's infamous place in history was sealed with the massacre of 500 to 700 Native men, women and children in 1644 in the Pound Ridge area. Underhill had taken advantage of a large gathering of the Native people assembled for a corn festival, choosing that moment to strike with devastating consequences.

It is reported that Judge Samuel I. Rosenman, counselor to Governor, and later President, Franklin D. Roosevelt, owned a home on Cole Shears Road on the western end of Mt. Nimham during this period. He also served as a counselor to President Harry Truman, who reportedly visited him there during his presidency.

Around the mid-1950s, the need for fire watchers atop the tower was replaced by aerial observation. So New York State removed the lower section of the stairs leading to the cabin. The log cabin used by the fire watchers eventually fell into disrepair.

Willis Booth and his family were the last tenants in the old Townsend house on the Fairview Farm. By the mid-1950s the house was no longer habitable (Merritt).

1950-1953: Gerald Kirby Smalley, the great-grandson of Samuel and Mary Smalley from the western side of Mt. Nimham, near what is now the Clearpool Education Center, served as a corporal in the U.S. Army during the Korean War.

Illustration 18: Woody Cornell's Ski Slope Equipment Shed *(Photo by author)*

1952: On January 2nd, George C. Whipple Jr. married JoeAnn Feeley at Our Lady of the Lake Roman Catholic Church in Lake Carmel. The newlyweds celebrated their wedding reception at the Gipsy Trail Club. They would make their home at the Pine View Farm on Gipsy Trail Road along the eastern base of the mountain. The Whipple family traces their lineage back to

Captain John Whipple, who served under Commodore Abraham Whipple, another relative, and the hero of the Battle of Narragansett Bay, in which the first British ship of the American Revolution was sunk. He is most famous for responding to the wanted poster issued by Captain James Wallace, who campaigned, "You Abraham Whipple on the 10th of June 1772 burned his majesty's vessel the Gaspee and I will hang you at the yard arm!" To which Whipple responded, "Sir, always catch a man before you hang him" (PreservePutnam.org).

George C. Whipple Jr. was a public relations executive at Benton and Bowles, the advertising agency that created the famous "Don't squeeze the Charmin" advertising campaign. Mr. Whipple licensed his name for use by the main character in the commercials for one dollar. The commercial, which was originally only scheduled to run for six months on the west coast, became the longest running ad campaign in the history of television.

Illustration 19: Arsenic Mine Insignia (l.) & Stationery (r.) *(Courtesy of the Rickert-Shatz Family)*

1953: On April 12th, Walter Niles Dean passed away at the age of 64 in Brooklyn. He was the son of Colonel Fremont and Margaret Clark Dean. Walter grew up on Mt. Nimham on the farm previously owned by his uncle, William Niles Dean, located on the access road leading up to the fire tower. He was laid to rest in the Raymond Hill Cemetery along with the other members of the Dean family.

1955: Stephen Townsend, the grandson of Stephen and son of Judge Coleman S. Townsend, passed away on March 10th at the age of 76. Stephen Townsend was a miner, stone-mason, and farmer, living off of Smokey Hollow Court, and later Clearpool Road, and had built the John Hayes house on East Boyds Road, among others. He also reportedly built the explosives bunker located on the Fairview Farm, adjacent to the NYS DEC parking area on the mountain. He was laid to rest in his family's plot in the First Baptist Church of Kent Cliffs Cemetery.

1960: In this year, New York State passed "The Park and Recreation Land Acquisition Act," followed by the Environmental Quality Bond Acts of 1972 and 1986. These laws contained provisions for the acquisition of lands to be managed for multiple uses and added to the State Forest system. These lands would serve multiple purposes involving the conservation and development of natural resources, including the preservation of scenic areas, watershed protection, forestry and recreation.

As visitors to the mountain during this period, local residents Wilma and Jim Baker remembered seeing the old Townsend farmhouse and barn in the area which is now used as the NYS DEC parking area on Mt. Nimham Court. The house was located just to the north of the stream and wetland area, on the western side of the parking area. The old barn was located across what is now the parking lot, to the east of the house. These locations and layouts are consistent with the historical maps of the 1800s. Inside the barn was stored an old classic Chrysler Airflow automobile, circa mid-1930s (see Illustration 20).

Soon after, local resident Ralph Merritt was hired by New York State to tear down the old Townsend house on the Fairview Farm, which had become unhabitable. Mr. Merritt recalled that the two-story shingled house had its gable-side facing down the mountain, adjacent to the man-made pond. Next to the pond was found a potato patch and vegetable garden. The red barn was located just across the driveway, to the east of the house.

Ralph Merritt, who is also a World War II veteran and married Mt. Nimham resident Alice Adams (the daughter of Percy Adams), also built the improved road which connected Clearpool Road with the top of Cole Shears Road. It is along this roadway where the stone chamber, which was labeled as "ruins" on the 1854 map, is found. Across from this chamber is found an impressive collection of rock slabs which New York City mined to build many of the stone fences found around the reservoirs. This was once part of the Smalley farm from the late 1700s throughout the 1800s. Mr. Merritt also performed numerous construction jobs over the years for Bill Pettey, who was associated with the Clearpool Camp.

Even though they no longer owned the property, the Townsend family would still gather on the mountain for annual picnics, enjoying the beautiful views, for many years to come.

1965: Stephen Kenneth ("Ken") Townsend married Ella Hyatt Pombo in this year. She was the widow of Joseph Pombo, and a longtime resident of Whang Hollow on Schrade and Farmers Mills Roads. They would make their home on the same property where the Robinsontown Schoolhouse (Schoolhouse No. 4) had been located, on the northeast corner of Schrade and Farmers Mills Roads. Ella Hyatt Pombo had lived in the old schoolhouse with her three children by her first marriage for many years following the death of her first husband. Ken Townsend was a direct descendant of the Townsend family from Mt. Nimham, and was the great-great-great grandson of the patriot Lt. Col. Elijah Townsend, and served as the Town of Kent Highway Supervisor for many years.

Bill Adams, the son of Percy Adams, served our country during the Vietnam War with great distinction and honors. He was the sole survivor of his squad, who were engaged in an intense firefight with Viet Cong guerillas. The Adams family had lived on the Fairview Farm on Mt. Nimham in the 1930s and 1940s.

1966: The U.S. Geologic Survey team installed two benchmarks on the top of Mt. Nimham near the fire tower (see Illustration 21). These benchmarks were cemented into holes drilled into two rock outcrops, with Benchmark No. 1 located to the southwest of the tower, and Benchmark No. 2 placed to the northwest of the tower. The USGS determined that the elevation of Benchmark No. 1 measured 1,276 feet above sea level, and Benchmark No. 2's elevation reached 1,273 feet. This is in marked contrast to the previously

Illustration 20: Remains of the Chrysler Airflow *(Photo by author)*

published USGS maps which indicated that the mountaintop reached an elevation of 1,426 feet, which would have made it the highest point in

Putnam County. Recent GPS readings, indicating an elevation of between 1,284 and 1,350 feet above sea level at the highest point, suggests that the truth lies somewhere in between the extremes represented by the USGS estimates.

1968: Gil Cryinghawk Tarbox, of the Passamaquoddy and Micmac nations (Algonquin tribes whose homelands included the areas of Maine and southern Canada), served our country with distinction in Vietnam in this year. Mr. Tarbox lives along the northwestern edge of the mountain today, and is an extremely active preservationist and representative of the ways of the Native people.

1970: The New York State Department of Environmental Conservation instituted a reforesting program, which included the Mt. Nimham Multiple Use Area. The DEC-run program introduced an incursion of noxious alien species such as multi-flora rose and Japanese barberry, which have become invasive species on the mountain.

Illustration 21: USGS Benchmarks on Mt. Nimham (*Photos by author*)

1976: On April 2nd, Clarence James Townsend passed away at the age of 74. He was the brother of Ken Townsend, and the son of Stephen and Anna Augusta Light Townsend. He was also the great-great-great grandson of the patriot Elijah Townsend. Clarence Townsend served with distinction as Historian for the Town of Kent.

1980s: Mt. Nimham residents Joan Rickert and Evan Shatz recalled that the old Townsend barn, located on the southwestern corner of what is now the NYS DEC parking area on Mt. Nimham Court, had finally collapsed from the elements and the passage of time. The old barn wood was retrieved by other local residents in the hope that one day it would find another life. The Rickert-Shatz family own the beautiful Woody Cornell A-frame chalet on the lower eastern side of the mountain (Rickert-Shatz Family oral history).

The fire warden's cabin (see Illustration 22), located at the top of the mountain near the fire tower, which had been abandoned following the discontinuance of the fire watchers in the mid-1950s, became the victim of arson by vandals during this time period. The site of the cabin is now an open field located adjacent to the fire tower. The scattered foundation stones and a nearby midden are the only remnants of this structure today.

Illustration 22: Musician David Amram performing on the front porch of the fire warden's cabin in 1987 *(Photo courtesy of George Baum, and Jim and Wilma Baker)*

1990: The Clearpool Education Center, located on the western side of the mountain where the Smalley family once lived, redefined itself to become a year-round campus for its public school partners, as well as for other educational and human service organizations.

1994: Vandals destroyed the cabin atop the Mt. Nimham Fire Tower, and damaged the remaining wooden steps leading up to the cabin. The Kent Conservation Advisory Committee and PLAN-Kent, under the leadership of Ray Singer, Dr. George Baum, and James and Wilma Baker, formed a group called "The Friends of Mt. Nimham" to begin raising funds for its restoration. They sold inscribed nameplates which were placed on each step leading up to the top, and raised additional funding from other private and governmental sources.

1995: Starting around 1995, additional incursive vegetation began making significant inroads on the mountain and within the forest. These include garlic mustard and oriental bittersweet.

1997: On April 27th in Southfield, Massachusetts, Stephen Wood Cornell, age 88, passed away. "Woody" Cornell was once the owner of the Carmel Lumber Yard, which later became Lloyd's and finally Dill's, on Route 52. Woody Cornell also built the A-frame house and nearby ski slope, complete with lights and a J-bar, on the lower eastern side of Mt. Nimham, adjacent to the old "Brown's Silver Mine Hole." A World War II veteran, Cornell was laid to rest in the Raymond Hill Cemetery.

Mr. Cornell, though being a direct descendant of the infamous Captain John Underhill, was always very supportive of memorializing Chief Nimham for his life and sacrifice at the Battle of Kingsbridge.

1999: The Nimham Mountain Singers, a group of local vocalists with the goal of fostering, preserving and rediscovering traditional Native American beliefs, values and spirituality, was formed in this year. The group consisted of Bill *'Panther Warrior'*, Penny *'Painted Pony'*, Brooke *'Wolf That Runs With Pony'*, Wendy *'Walks Soft'*, and Gil *'Cryinghawk'*. They sing and share with their communities northern woodland songs, mostly of the first people, the Algonquin speaking peoples, which includes the Nochpeem who called the mountain their home. This organization performs at the annual Daniel Nimham Pow Wow held at the Putnam County Veteran's Memorial Park, located in the shadow of the mountain, an extraordinary event which they also organize each year. They also perform at schools, civic events and other pow wows, and offer a complete educational program of drumming, traditional songs and dances, and Wappinger (Nochpeem) cultural history designed for children and adults. Through their good work, the culture and traditions of the "first people" are being preserved and shared for the education and enjoyment of generations to come. They employ an extremely inclusive approach, which brings together the descendants of the first people with descendants of the immigrants who followed later. In doing so, they have fostered an environment of cooperation and mutual respect, and have helped to create a renewed appreciation for the ways of the Native people, who have always respected and revered the natural world around us.

Chapter 7

Mount Nimham in the 21st Century

As the residents of the Mount Nimham area entered the 21st century, they had every reason to believe that their beautiful mountain would continue to flourish, having become public land available to all for a variety of recreational purposes. However, as all their forbearers had learned over the previous centuries, new challenges and threats would continue to present themselves. And as the availability of the world's resources came into question, and a period of excessive consumption and speculation went bust, the conservationist ways of their Native American predecessors would foster a revived appreciation for those who preceded them here . . .

2000: Ken Townsend and his wife, Ella Hyatt Pombo Townsend, were interviewed by Katherine Kane regarding the history of the Mt. Nimham fire tower. Ken was the great-grandson of Stephen Townsend, the long-time owner of the Fairview Farm on the southeastern face of the mountain, epicentered at the intersection of Mt. Nimham Court and Coles Mills Road. At its peak, it was composed of 550 acres, extending from Route 301 near the Town Highway Garage to just north of the fire tower. Ken could trace his heritage back to his great-great-great grandfather, Lt. Col. Elijah Townsend, a patriot from the Revolution and one of the original settlers on the mountain. Today, remnants of the farm can still be seen on the northern hillside adjoining the DEC parking area at the intersection of Mt. Nimham Court and Coles Mills Road.

When Ken was a youngster visiting his grandfather's farm, which was later owned by his uncle, in the 1920s and 1930s, he personally observed the remains of the Nochpeem forts at the top and western face of Mt. Nimham. He reported that at least a few of the lodges still had roofs on them, more than 200 years after their construction. However, during the Depression and the CCC public works program, the lodges were bulldozed while constructing the road leading to the top of the mountain and the fire tower. This first-hand, independent confirmation from a direct descendant of the documented owners of a long-established farm on Mt. Nimham serves as indisputable proof of the importance of Mt. Nimham to the local Native American Indians, which lasted for thousands of years.

Also occurring in the year 2000, the Keropian family moved into the Townsend/Heady house on Gipsy Trail Road, just south of the DEC parking area and directly across from the mountain. Michael Keropian, a world-class sculptor, soon became fascinated with the mountain and its namesake. He began researching the life of Chief Nimham, and in 2001 he visited, studied and compared the native crania at the Smithsonian Institute in Washington DC. He also found a Native American death mask at the New York Historical Society. He combined this information with the books he had researched and the descriptions of the Native people. This inspiring process, in terms of both a scientific and spiritual journey, led to the creation of his model sculpture of the great chief (see Illustration 2). This work of art captured the typical dress of the Native people, including the bear claw necklace, and shows the Chief holding an Indian Deed, which Nimham had so effectively used in his attempt to regain a portion of the Wappinger ancestral homeland. It is the great hope of the people of Kent that this statue of Chief Daniel Nimham will one day grace the Wappinger Memorial, in addition to the entrance of the Kent Town Hall Complex on Route 52.

2003: Stephen Kenneth Townsend, the son of Stephen Townsend and husband of Ella Hyatt Pombo Townsend, passed away at the age of 97 on April 25th. "Ken" Townsend served as Highway Supervisor for the Town of Kent for many years. His recollections of his boyhood visits to his grandfather's, and later his uncle's farm on Mt. Nimham, provided direct, eyewitness testimony to the Nochpeem legacy on the mountain. Mr. Townsend was also a proud World War II veteran.

In September, the New York State DEC formally proposed the establishment of a model forest on up to 415 acres of Mt. Nimham, to be located on the southern and eastern portions of the mountain, including all of Coles Mills Road. The original sites of the Townsend and Russell farms dating back to pre-Revolution days, in addition to a portion of the Nochpeem ancestral homeland hunting grounds, would be included in the model forest area. The plan would involve the logging of trees to thin the forest, and the application of herbicides to remove invasive ground plants in an attempt to accelerate the evolution toward an old growth forest. The State plan included having the Army Corps of Engineers "rehabilitate" the Revolutionary era trail, Coles Mills Road, into a wide all-weather road to accommodate logging trucks and tour buses. Once completed, the State would remove 40% to 60% of the biomass over 87 acres of forest using tree thinning, herbicides, fire and a 15-acre clear-cut. Studies would then be conducted, and if the project was deemed successful, it would expand to 415 acres.

It should be noted that 415 acres represents approximately 40% of the entire Mt. Nimham Multiple Use Area, which covers both the mountain itself and the old Brown-Northrup farms to the east in Whang Hollow. DEC Forester Jeff Weigert said, *"Forest management promotes the growth of the biggest and best trees, and there is removal of wood which isn't as hardy. The focus here is on water quality, and managing the forest properly improves the quality of the watershed."* The DEC said they had completed two years of baseline study and research on the mountain at a cost of almost $300,000 in preparation for the beginning of logging operations, and they didn't want to see that money go to waste.

The plan was met with immediate opposition from the local community. Local residents Penny Ann Osborn and Jeff Green helped to mobilize opposition to the plan, which soon included local historians, community groups, politicians, and a number of biologists and botanists, who argued that the forest should mature naturally just as the original old growth forest had developed. Croton Watershed Clean Water Coalition (CWCWC) President Dr. Marian Rose, in a December 2003 letter to the DEC, wrote: *"This proposal defies both common sense and logic. DEC has not provided the public with any proof whatsoever that clear-cutting 15 acres, thinning the forest up to 60% and applying herbicides to clear underbrush will not harm water quality in the nearby reservoir, let alone enhance it. DEC's emphasis is on the "biggest and best trees", i.e., those that provide the biggest return as lumber; it is not on providing protection for the reservoir or habitat for the wildlife"* (PlanPutnam).

Dr. Parker Gambino, an entomologist from Southeast, stated, *"The DEC, through its management practices of the past years has already caused great damage to the Nimham Mountain unit. The road to the [fire] tower is clearly the avenue for incursion of noxious alien species such as multiflora rose and barberry. Within the last decade, there have also been significant inroads made by garlic mustard and oriental bittersweet. If DEC is serious about forestry, perhaps ecologically sound management of invasive plants would be a good place to start"* (PlanPutnam).

In addition, local historians opposed the plan due to the likelihood of there being numerous Native American burial sites across the mountain, given their lengthy history and association with the mountain over thousands of years. Historians were also concerned with the potential loss of historic artifacts covering both the Native American and early European-American settlers, including many patriots from the War of Independence. In December, the Kent Town Board unanimously passed a resolution opposing the DEC's plan, and the local State government representatives added their support in questioning the DEC's plan as well. However, the DEC continued to work on modified plans for a model forest, promising that this issue would continue to develop for many years to come (See Appendices D and E regarding New York State Statutes covering Historic Areas and the impacts from State Agencies' actions).

2004: A project was undertaken by the Kent Conservation Advisory Committee (KCAC) to investigate the status of the old town roads, including Coles Mills Road, which had become "paths in the woods." According to the New York State Highway Act of 1909 and its amendments, the only way a road can be formally abandoned is through a majority vote of the local governing authority to formally abandon the road. Without such a formal abandonment order, the road is presumed to remain a town road. As a member of the KCAC, this author requested that the Town Clerk perform a search of town records to determine which of these old roads had actually been formally abandoned by the Kent Town Board over the years.

2005: The Kent Conservation Advisory Committee and PLAN-Kent completed its restoration of the steel fire tower originally erected by the CCC and New York State in 1940 (see Illustration 23). The restoration took five years and cost more than $30,000. Equipped with new steel stairs and a restored cabin, Kent residents and other visitors were once again able to behold the breathtaking 75 mile-round views from the top of the 90-foot high tower, ranging from the Manhattan skyline to the south, the Shawangunks and Catskills to the northwest, and the Berkshires to the northeast. An organization called "The Friends of Mt. Nimham" was formed and granted stewardship of this magnificent structure. The Mt. Nimham Fire Tower is listed on the National Historic Lookout Register.

Based upon a search of town records completed by the Kent Town Clerk's Office, as requested by the Kent Conservation Advisory Committee, it was determined that there was no known formal abandonment resolution on file for Coles Mills Road, and thus had never been formally abandoned by the Kent Town Board, per the abandonment requirements of the New York State Highway Act of 1909 and its amendments. Without a formal order of abandonment approved by the Town Board, the road was presumed to have remained a town road. This designation as a town road made it virtually impossible for the DEC to implement its logging plans, which had included the need to widen Coles Mills Road for use in its logging operations.

Sometime following the news of the town's continued role in relation to this historic road, and in concert with the ongoing opposition of local environmentalists, the New York State DEC eventually "unofficially" dropped its plan to log Mt. Nimham. The chief reason cited was the concern surrounding the modification of Coles Mills Road. Local activists and historians had argued that critical cultural and historic resources located along this road would be irreversibly damaged by the DEC's plan to "improve" the road to allow for the heavy machinery needed to accomplish its logging plans.

2006: On July 2nd, the Gold Star Mothers' Memorial was dedicated at the Putnam County Veteran's Park, in the shadow of Mt. Nimham. Created by sculptor Andrew L. Chernak, and coordinated by Peter Allegretta, this moving remembrance salutes the mothers of all the patriots who made the supreme sacrifice for our country.

Illustration 23: The Restored Fire Tower on Mt. Nimham (*Photo by author*)

2007: Located just east of Mt. Nimham on the old Northrup farm, the Wappinger Memorial was dedicated on Veterans Day, November 11th of this year (see Illustration 24). Gil Cryinghawk Tarbox, of the Passamaquoddy and Micmac, and a Vietnam veteran, organized and planned the updated memorial, which had originally been designated as a memorial to Chief Nimham. The original monument was designed and implemented by Penny Painted Pony Osborn and the late Richard Muscarella, the former president of the Kent Historical Society and former Putnam County Historian. But Mr. Tarbox recognized that in addition to memorializing Chief Nimham, it was important to remember the Wappinger Confederacy tribes, and Native American Indian veterans, who had never been adequately recognized in this, their ancestral homeland. The updated memorial includes both the original monument to Chief Nimham in addition to 12 stones, with the name and location of each Wappinger tribe inscribed upon them, placed in a circle built into the original memorial. This inspiring monument serves as an ever present reminder of our Native American Indian predecessors who called this area their home for thousands of years before the arrival of the Europeans.

Illustration 24: Wappinger Memorial Dedication *(Photo by author)*

2008: Based upon an application submitted by this author on January 31st, the farm site of the patriot Lt. Thomas Russell, located on Coles Mills Road, was officially designated as an inventoried New York State historic archaeological site by the State Historic Preservation Office. This action will help protect the old farm site, Coles Mills Road, and the surrounding forest

126

from disturbances caused by projects implemented under the direction, review, or funding by New York State agencies and departments. Additional applications to designate the Smalley/Townsend and Brown/Dean farms as New York State inventoried archaeological sites have also been filed and are pending approval as of this writing.

In September, an historical marker was erected by the Town of Kent, under the direction of Town Historian Richard T. Othmer Jr., at the corner of Gipsy Trail Road and Mt. Nimham Court (see Illustration 25). This marker acknowledges the role of the patriot Chief Daniel Nimham during the War of Independence. It also stands in marked contrast to the New York State DEC sign, pictured in the background, which incorrectly spelled his name, despite repeated requests over the years to have it corrected, to no avail.

Illustration 25: Town of Kent Historical Marker for Mount Nimham *(Photo by author)*

Today: The area once known as "Smalley Hill" is now named after the great Wappinger Sachem, and true American hero and patriot, Chief Daniel Nimham. It is a beautiful example of a "new growth" forest, maturing naturally, even though there are quite a few trees in excess of 100 years of age still standing proudly. Owned by the people of New York State (except for a northerly portion owned by the NYC DEP and the Gipsy Trail Club,

127

and the Clearpool Education Center to the west), and managed by the New York State Department of Environmental Conservation, this beautiful and sacred mountain is enjoyed by hikers, mountain bikers, and naturalists year-round, and by hunters in-season. Native Americans from many different tribes still come to visit the land upon which Chief Nimham came to proclaim all that could be seen from its peak to be part of the Wappinger ancestral homeland.

Although most of the original farms on Mt. Nimham have passed into history, there is still abundant evidence of their existence. The Townsend's Fairview Farm can be identified by the remaining stone explosives bunker (see Illustration 28), which was also used as a smokehouse, the remains of a stonewalled structure which served as a chicken coop, and the stream culvert located near the intersection of Mt. Nimham Court and Coles Mills Road. Just below the DEC parking area one will find an old stone chimney, which may have been the chimney for the Townsend farm house. A little further below is found the remains of an old rusted automobile, which is believed to be the 1930s Chrysler Air-Flow that was once stored in the old barn (Illustration 20). Reminders of the farming activities on the Fairview Farm are found with the old rusting farm machinery used by the Townsends and their tenants to plow, cultivate, and harvest their fields (Illustration 26).

Illustration 26: Townsend "Fairview Farm" Remnant *(Photo by author)*

Evidence of the Thomas and Morris Russell farm exists with the stone storehouse enclosure of three walls on Coles Mills Road heading south toward Route 301 (see Illustration 27). Stone steps leading to the house site are found directly across the road (Illustration 28), with other remnants of an old well, cistern, or privy. Another corbelled stone chamber, partially collapsed, resides just a bit to the north adjacent to the road itself, facing away from the roadway.

Illustration 27: Russell Farm Storehouse on Coles Mills Road *(Photo by author)*

Illustration 28: Russell Farm, With Stone Walkway Leading to the House Site *(Photo by author)*

The "Silver Mine Hole" is still in existence on the lower eastern side of the mountain, located on private property, although it is mostly filled in. "Brown's Quarry" can still be seen from Gipsy Trail Road, just south of Mt. Nimham Court.

At the northern end of the mountain, there are numerous stone remnants still remaining from the patriot Samuel Hawkins - Henry Light - Isaac Parker - Harry Maynard farm (see Illustration 29), including the stone chamber, the old well, the barn area and another structure labeled as a "milk house" on the 1854 R.F. O'Connor map. Their fields stretched to the rear, western side of Stockholm Hill.

Illustration 29: The Corbelled Stone Chamber from the Hawkins/Light/ Parker/Maynard Farm on Maynard Road *(Photo by author)*

Along the eastern base of the mountain, the "Pine View Farm" continues on as a glimpse into the area's past. Mrs. JoeAnn Feeley Whipple, the daughter of Robert Stanton Feeley, and her son, George C. Whipple III, have made this farm the home to more than 10 different breeds of early American farm animals. Included are Randall Lineback Cattle, American Jacob Sheep, Pilgrim Geese, Indian Runner Ducks, and Narragansett Turkey.

The road originally known as Cole Shears Road is now called Cole Shears Court. The windy dirt road ends at the top of a long hill, one of the many "arms" of the mountain. A corbelled stone chamber located on the old Wixon farm stands directly adjacent to the roadway. Smalley Corners Road also ends prematurely as compared to the maps of the 1800s, with the extension gated off, now merely a trail in the woods. Clear Pool Road has also been shortened from its original length. The site listed on the maps of the 1800s as "Mrs. Smalley and Sons" (Mary Smalley) still exists on this road, and is evidenced by the old log cabin/carriage house and barn found there today. Part of the original road is now just a trail along the western side of the mountain. Another stone chamber can be found along this old road, which was curiously labeled as "ruins" on the 1854 map.

Coles Mills Road, which runs down the southern spine of the mountain, continues to be a town road, having apparently never been formally abandoned by the Town of Kent. Reported to originally have been a Native trail, this historic road has been home to so many patriots over the years.

Reminders of William Niles Dean's presence on the mountain also continue to be evident (see Illustrations 30 and 31). The remains of his house on the road up to the fire tower, the path found on maps entitled "Uncle WN's Path", the well and stone enclosure all serve as enduring reminders of

Illustration 30: Entryway to the Dean House *(Photo by author)*

his life on the mountain.

The extensive stone fences built by these farmers to mark off their fields and contain their animals are still seen throughout the mountain today. Despite its steep slopes, the curving ridgelines left by the glaciers produced terraced ridge lines that supported farming activities throughout the 1700s, 1800s, and into the early 1900s. Even while walking up the main road to the fire tower, one can see how these farmers utilized the contours of the land to the best of their abilities to create their fields. The top, western, and southern sides of the mountain are where one can see this most clearly today. These stone fences serve as constant reminders of these farms, with each stone having been touched by the very hands of these early settlers and patriots sometime over the past 250 years.

Paths carved and utilized by the Nochpeem and the original farmers to access their fields and connect with their neighbors are still used and enjoyed by hikers and mountain bikers today. Many of our early town roads were originally Native footpaths that were reused by the early settlers. The mountain itself is honeycombed with numerous trails and old cart-paths that allow hikers to circumnavigate the mountain, and discover the rippled landscape as one valley or gorge merges with another. Hikers are rewarded with both the scenic views from its summit and along the western high ridges, as well as the prehistoric gorges and mini-valleys found within the mountain's inner-folds. Amazing rock formations, boulder fields, and glacial boulders and erratics can be found nearly everywhere one walks today on the mountain.

Illustration 31: The Corbelled Stone Chamber on the Brown/Dean Farm (l.), and the Explosives Bunker/Smokehouse on the Fairview Farm (r.) *(Photos by author)*

These early inhabitants could watch the shadow of the mountain diminish

132

over the western side as the sun rose, and later enjoy the view of the extending shadow across the eastern valley as the sun set (Illustration 32). As we enjoy these same views today, we can only imagine all the hopes, dreams, and heartaches of these early inhabitants of the mountain that accompanied the great natural beauty that abounds.

Illustration 32: Shadow of Mt. Nimham Extending Across Whang Hollow Toward Pine Pond *(Photo by author)*

As previously noted, the historian William S. Pelletreau perhaps best captured the historic and cultural significance of this mountain to the people of Kent and Putnam County, when he wrote in 1886:

"A person who stands on the high land in Carmel, south of Lake Gleneida, sees far to the northwest, three lofty mountains that tower above all the country round. To the middle peak, which is the highest, we have given the name of the last Sachem of the tribe that once ruled all the lands that can be seen from its highest summit: and we trust that in honor of his valor, and of the faith sealed with his blood, on the field where he fought for the liberty of America, it will bear to all future time the name of Mount Nimham" (86).

And if one listens very carefully on a still evening on the mountain, perhaps they will hear the prayers and songs of the great Sachem who once proclaimed that all that could be seen from its peak, was the ancient ancestral homeland of his people (Osborn; Dacquino).

And as the presidential tribute for fallen service men and women, which exemplifies the expression of a grateful nation for the Mt. Nimham patriots who have made the ultimate sacrifice for their country, so poignantly states:

"They stand in the unbroken line of patriots who have dared to die that freedom might live, and grow, and increase its blessings. Freedom lives, and through it, they live – in a way that humbles the undertakings of most men."

We will always remember and honor their sacrifices in defense of our enduring freedom, these many patriots of Mount Nimham!

Appendix A:

The Pledge

(Reprinted from William Blake's 1849 *History of Putnam County*)

"Persuaded that the salvation of the rights and liberties of America depend, under God, on the firm union of its inhabitants in a vigorous prosecution of the measures necessary for its safety, and convinced of the necessity of preventing anarchy and confusion which attend a dissolution of the powers of government, We, the Freemen, Freeholders, and Inhabitants of Duchess, being greatly alarmed at the avowed design of the Ministry to raise a revenue in America, and shocked by the bloody scene now acting in Massachusetts Bay, do in the most solemn manner resolve never to become slaves, and do associate, under all the ties of religion, honor, and love to our country, to adopt and endeavor to carry into execution whatsoever measures may be recommended by the Continental Congress, or resolved upon by our Provincial Convention, for the purpose of preserving our constitution and of opposing the several arbitrary acts of the British Parliament, until a reconciliation between Great Britain and America, on constitutional principles (which we most ardently desire) can be obtained; and that we will in all things follow the advice of our General Committee respecting the purposes aforesaid, the preservation of peace and good order and the safety of individuals and property."

Appendix B:

Population of the Town of Kent

(Courtesy of the Putnam County Historian's Office, as transcribed from the U.S. Census)

1800: 1,661
1810: 1,811
1820: 1,801
1830: 1,931
1840: 1,830
1850: 1,557
1860: 1,479
1870: 1,547
1880: 1,361
1890: 1,147
1900: 1,026
1910:   968
1920:   696
1930:   770
1940: 1,546
1950: 2,146
1960: 3,924
1970: 8,106
1980: 12,443
1990: 13,183
2000: 14,009

Appendix C:

The Mills Used by the Mount Nimham Area Farmers

1) Coles Mills: Gristmill, sawmill & carding mill, owned by the Cole family

2) Boyd's Corners: Sawmill, just northwest of Platt Parker's store (now the Kent Cliffs Deli)

3) Farmers Mills: Gristmill, sawmill & carding mill

4) Nichols Street, on the farm of Henry Nichols (where Reservoir D is currently located), sawmill and brickyard

5) Parker's Mills, located west of Nimham Road, along the outlet from Farmers' Mills and the inlet to the West Branch of the Croton River

6) Dean Pond outlet, northwest of Dean Pond: Sawmill, believed to be owned by James Cole

7) Milltown Road, northwest of White Pond: Sawmill, owned by Charles & Eli Mead

8) Old Ludingtonville Road/Horsepound Road: Gristmill & sawmill, owned by the Ludington family

Appendix D:

Article 31 of NYS Legal Code Regarding Declaration of Policy Regarding Historic Areas

§ 31.03 Declaration of policy. The urban and regional areas of the state are rich in cultural and natural resources of statewide significance associated with our growth and attainments over time. These resources offer educational, inspirational and recreational benefits for present and future generations. It is hereby declared to be the policy of the state to preserve these resources through their identification, interpretation, development and use in a system made up of state designated heritage areas including urban cultural parks and heritage corridors. It is further the policy of the state to improve and coordinate the plans, functions, powers and programs of the state, as they affect its urban and regional cultural and natural resources, in cooperation with the federal government, regions, local governments and other public and private organizations and concerned individuals.

Appendix E:

Article 14 of New York State Law Regarding State Agency Activities Affecting Historic or Cultural Property

§ 14.09 State agency activities affecting historic or cultural property; notice and comment. 1. As early in the planning process as may be practicable and prior to the preparation or approval of the final design or plan of any project undertaken by a state agency, or prior to the funding of any project by a state agency or prior to an action of approval or entitlement of any private project by a state agency, the agency's preservation officer shall give notice, with sufficient documentation, to and consult with the commissioner concerning the impact of the project if it appears that any aspect of the project may or will cause any change, beneficial or adverse, in the quality of any historic, architectural, archeological, or cultural property that is listed on the national register of historic places or property listed on the state register or is determined to be eligible for listing on the state register by the commissioner. Generally, adverse impacts occur under conditions which include but are not limited to (a) destruction or alteration of all or part of a property; (b) isolation or alteration of its surrounding environment; (c) introduction of visual, audible, or atmospheric elements that are out of character with the property or alter its setting; or (d) neglect of property resulting in its deterioration or destruction. Every agency shall fully explore all feasible and prudent alternatives and give due consideration to feasible and prudent plans which avoid or mitigate adverse impacts on such property. In the event that the agency has filed or will file with the department of environmental conservation, with respect to that contemplated project, a draft environmental impact statement pursuant to the provisions of article eight of the environmental conservation law, it shall provide a copy thereof to the commissioner and the chairman of the board and shall also supply such further information as the commissioner may request. This section shall not apply to a state project that is necessary to prevent an immediate and imminent threat to life or property. 2. The commissioner shall undertake a review and make comment within thirty days of receipt of notice, with sufficient documentation, of a proposed project as to whether or not such proposed project may have an adverse impact on any property that is listed on the national register of historic places or on the state register or is determined to be eligible for the state register by the commissioner. The comment shall be put on file and shall be available to the public on request. If it is determined that a project may have an adverse impact on such property, the commissioner shall so notify the agency in writing. Upon receipt of such notification from the commissioner, the agency shall immediately contact the commissioner for the purpose of exploring alternatives which would avoid or mitigate adverse impacts to such property consistent with the policy and provisions of this article and other provisions of law relating to historic preservation. To the fullest extent practicable, it is the responsibility of every state agency, consistent with other provisions of law, to avoid or mitigate adverse impacts to registered property or property determined eligible for listing on the state register by the commissioner. In order to avoid inconsistency or duplication in review functions, the commissioner shall establish procedures in accordance with other provisions of this section whereby reviews conducted under this section are coordinated with the reviews of project or plan proposals under other provisions of law and regulation. When a project is being reviewed pursuant to section one hundred six of the national historic preservation act of 1966, the procedures of this section shall not apply and any review or comment by the commissioner and the board on such project shall be within the framework or procedures of the section one hundred six review. The commissioner shall issue an annual report outlining state agency actions on which comment had been requested or issued under this section. Proposed alternatives and results of the review process shall be included in said annual report.

Appendix F:

"The Gipsy Trail"
by Rudyard Kipling
(1892)

The white moth to the closing bine,
  The bee to the opened clover,
And the gipsy blood to the gipsy blood
  Ever the wide world over.

Ever the wide world over, lass,
  Ever the trail held true,
Over the world and under the world,
  And back at the last to you.

Out of the dark of the gorgio camp,
  Out of the grime and the grey
(Morning waits at the end of the world),
  Gipsy, come away!

The wild boar to the sun-dried swamp,
  The red crane to her reed,
And the Romany lass to the Romany lad,
  By the tie of a roving breed.

The pied snake to the rifted rock,
  The buck to the stony plain,
And the Romany lass to the Romany lad,
  And both to the road again.

Both to the road again, again!
  Out on a clean sea-track --
Follow the cross of the gipsy trail
  Over the world and back!

Follow the Romany patteran
  North where the blue bergs sail,
And the bows are grey with the frozen spray,
  And the masts are shod with mail.

Follow the Romany patteran
  Sheer to the Austral Light,
Where the besom of God is the wild South wind,
  Sweeping the sea-floors white.

Follow the Romany patteran
  West to the sinking sun,
Till the junk-sails lift through the houseless drift.
  And the east and west are one.

Follow the Romany patteran
  East where the silence broods
By a purple wave on an opal beach
  In the hush of the Mahim woods.

"The wild hawk to the wind-swept sky,
  The deer to the wholesome wold,
And the heart of a man to the heart of a maid,
  As it was in the days of old."

The heart of a man to the heart of a maid --
  Light of my tents, be fleet.
Morning waits at the end of the world,
  And the world is all at our feet!

Appendix G:

Origins of the Corbelled Stone Chambers

Corbelled stone chambers (i.e., those covered with rock roof slabs with the side walls angled inward toward each other) can be found within the Mt. Nimham area, as well as throughout the town of Kent and Putnam County. There are a total of seven corbelled stone chambers on the mountain itself. One is located on Mt. Nimham Court, at the Smalley/Brown/Dean farm location. There is also an explosives bunker (not to be confused with a corbelled chamber) located on the Fairview Farm owned by the Townsend family, adjacent to the DEC parking area. Another corbelled chamber is found on Coles Mills Road on the old Russell farm, which is partially collapsed. An additional chamber is found on Cole Shears Road at the old John and Wright Wixon farm site, with yet another to be found further down toward Clear Pool on "Old Clear Pool Road." Another chamber is located at the site of the Samuel Hawkins farm on Old Maynard Road, on the northern end of the mountain. Finally, there are two more corbelled chambers located near Clear Pool. It is widely believed that the early farmers used these structures as root cellars and ice houses, since the cool temperatures within offered a good storage place for their livestock feed, farm outputs and excess meat, in an age before electricity and refrigeration. In fact, it was often said that a farmer's wealth could be measured by the amount of ice he could produce and store.

But who built these chambers? While the vast majority of historians believe the early farmers are responsible for their construction, some scholars believe that other Europeans arrived in North America long before Columbus and Henry Hudson. It is known that the Celts were a well-organized sea power when Julius Caesar and his Roman Legions invaded the British Isles in 55 B.C. The Celts were noted as having sophisticated ocean-going vessels even at that time. Stone structures found in New Hampshire are believed, by these scholars, to have been Celtic temple observatories dedicated to their sun-god "Bel." Other structures in Vermont are theorized to have been similarly dedicated to Celtic gods and goddesses, with reports of ancient artifacts such as burial urns having been found (Fell).

Celtic passage tombs are great mounds of earth covering a womblike central chamber of large stones entered by a serpentine passage. *Newgrange* is the renowned passage tomb of Ireland whose otherwise dark central chamber is lit once a year by the dawn of sunlight at Winter Solstice. This tomb is nearly as large as a football field -- and it was built 1,000 years before the Great Pyramids of Egypt. While the presence of bones led early archeologists to believe that these were graves, it is clear from the womblike structure that they were in fact ceremonial chambers, much like gigantic sweat lodges into which the bundled bones of ancestors were brought for ceremony and perhaps storage. The astronomical features of these monuments link them to ceremonies honoring the yearly passage of time: the equinoxes, the solstices and the spiritually-powerful midpoints between them, which are the high Celtic holidays of Imbolc, Beltain, Llammas and Samain (Evans).

It has also been noted that when the Scandinavian Norsemen arrived around the tenth century, they found evidence of Irish and Welsh settlements. There is the legend of the Irish monk Brendan having journeyed to America in a hide-covered boat known as a coracle. There is also the story of the Culdees, a group from the ancient Celtic Church in Ireland, fleeing the sea raids of the still pagan Vikings, following Brendan's earlier route, seeking refuge first in Iceland, then Greenland, Newfoundland and finally, deep into North America. They then disappeared, perhaps giving rise to the traditions common to the Aztecs, Incas and Mayas, of visits by bearded white men.

Legends and traditions also persist that a Welsh Prince named Madog and his followers, fleeing from violence and bloodshed in Wales, escaped by ship and, using ancient Celtic maps and charts, crossed the Atlantic and landed on American soil at Mobile Bay in 1170 A.D. Moving inland, they built fortified settlements in Alabama, Georgia and Tennessee, giving rise to later claims of discovery of 'Welsh Indians' between the mid 1500's and early 1800's. George Catlin believed that he had traced the descendants of these Welsh settlers among the Mandan Indians, many of whom were blue-eyed and whose language contained elements of the Welsh language.

Other legends passed down through Native American Indian culture suggests that they may have used these stone chambers to store their dead during the winter months, when the ground was too frozen to dig proper burial places. However, some Native American scholars do not believe their ancestors would actually have built these structures, thus supporting the theory of early European involvement. There are also legends of early white men having been here using trade routes that were not Native American in origin.

Finally, there has been a recent discovery of rock walls existing under the Hudson River. Climatology experts claim that the last time the Hudson was shallow enough for such construction occurred approximately 3,000 years ago, long before Columbus and Henry Hudson.

One question that arises during this debate: If the early farmers built these "root cellars," why did they apparently copy the design and layout known to originate from the Celts? For example, why are so many of the chambers facing southeast, seemingly to capture the sun's rays during the de-facto sunrise on the solstice or equinox to project light directly toward the rear of the chamber? One possible explanation has to do with the origins of these farmers themselves. For example, the Mead family originated from Scotland, a one-time Celtic stronghold. Celtic traditions ran deep in many of these immigrants who came to the New World seeking freedom and opportunity. As these farmers constructed their root cellars, they may have relied on these traditions in designing and building their stone chambers, though not necessarily for religious purposes, since these settlers were Christian and did not worship the Celtic gods.

Other historians have found evidence of the existence of roaming construction gangs during the early and mid-1800s. It is believed these gangs specialized in the construction and repair of these stone structures and stone walls, thus supporting the root cellar/ice house position.

The 1854 R.F. O'Connor map of Kent shows a site curiously labeled "Ruins" on Old Cole Shears Road and Old Clear Pool Road, which turns out to be the location of an interesting stone chamber. The entrance to this chamber is offset, unlike most of the others in this area. Its impressive corbelling suggests a beehive-like design. If the early settlers did build these structures, why would this have been labeled as "ruins" as far back as 1854? This suggests the *possibility* that these structures are much older than the arrival of the European settlers in this area.

Regardless of one's opinion regarding the origins or uses of these structures, everyone agrees that they must be preserved for future generations, so they may have the opportunity, as we have, to study and debate their history.

Bibliography

Adams, Adelbert "Snookie". Oral History of Mt. Nimham and the Fairview Farm, Kent New York, 2009.

Baker, James and Wilma. Oral History of Mt. Nimham, Kent, New York, 2008.

Barnum, H.L. The Spy Unmasked: Memoirs of Enoch Crosby. Cincinnati: A. B. Roff, 1831.

Barrett Family Genealogy, Internet: http://barrett- genealogy.tripod.com/p_ 10.htm#3683, 2004.

Beers, Frederick W. Atlas of New York and Vicinity. New York: F.W. Beers, A.D. Ellis and G.G. Soule, 1868.

Beers, J.H. Commemorative Biographical Record of the Counties of Dutchess and Putnam, New York : Containing biographical sketches of prominent and representative citizens, and of many of the early settled families. Chicago : J.H. Beers & Co., 1897.

Behr, Bettymarie Light, "Houses of Worship," An Historic Biographical Profile of the Town of Kent, Putnam County, New York. Kent New York: Town of Kent Bicentennial Committee, 1976.

Blake, William J. The History of Putnam County, NY. New York: Baker & Scribner, 1849.

Boesch, Eugene J. "Native Americans of Putnam County." Internet: http://www.mahopaclibrary.org/localhistory/addendum.htm, 2003.

Brech, Martin. Stone Chambers of Putnam County, New York State. New York: The Society for the Preservation of Putnam County Antiquities and Greenways, George C. Whipple III, President, 2000.

Brewster High School Chapter of the National Honor Society. Today in History: Almanac of Putnam County. Brewster NY: Brewster Chapter of the National Honor Society, 1976.

Burr, David H. "Map of the Counties of Dutchess and Putnam." Albany: 1829 (reproduced 1839).

Cole Family Genealogy, found on Internet: http://www.angelfire.com /ny/chickened/colefamily.html

Conklin, Henry S. "Maps of Lots Sold by the New York Commissioners of Forfeitures, 1779-1786." Reproduced from the original forfeiture deeds, drafted by Henry S. Conklin, 1887. (Putnam County Historian's Office).

Dacquino, Vincent T. Hauntings of the Hudson River Valley. Charleston SC: Haunted America, 2007.

Deeds of the Town of Kent, Putnam County, New York. Putnam County Archives & Putnam County Historian's Office, 2004 - 2009.

Evans, Nancy Lee. Celtic Spirituality. Internet: http://www.alaska wellness.com/sept-oct01/celtic.htm, 2004.

Family Search, The Church of Jesus Christ of Latter-Day Saints, Internet: http://www.FamilySearch.org, 2004.

Fell, Barry. America B.C.: Ancient Settlers in the New World. New York: Pocket Books, 1989.

Fisher, Rev. Floyd B. They All Rest Together: Burial Sites of the Early Settlers--Southern Dutchess and Putnam Counties. Holmes NY: Floyd Fisher, 1972.

Flato, Mike, "Mines and Mining (in the Town of Kent)", An Historic Biographical Profile of the Town of Kent, Putnam County, New York, Town of Kent Bicentennial Committee, 1976.

Frazier, Patrick. The Mohicans of Stockbridge. Lincoln, NB: University of Nebraska Press, 1992.

Funk, Robert E. Recent Contributions to Hudson Valley Prehistory. Albany: University of the State of New York, 1976.

Greenwood, Lynn E. "The Putnam Sportsman." Putnam County Courier, 2007.

Grumet, Robert S. The Lenapes. New York: Chelsea House Publishers, 1989.

Grumet, Robert S. "Trade, War and Diplomacy." *Hudson Valley Magazine.*

February, 1991, pp. 15-17.

Grumet, Robert S. "The Nimhams of the Colonial Hudson Valley, 1667-1783." *The Hudson Valley Regional Review*, 9 (2) (September 1992): pp. 80-99.

Hodge, F.W. (ed.) Indian Notes and Monographs (Vol. II). New York: Museum of the American Indian, Heye Foundation, 1919-1920.

Illiano, Edward. Oral History and Investigations Regarding Mt. Nimham, Kent NY, 2005 – 2009.

Johnson, Willis Fletcher. Colonel Henry Ludington: A Memoir. New York: Printed by Colonel Ludington's grandchildren, Lavinia Elizabeth Ludington and Charles Henry Ludington, 1907.

Kane, Katherine. "Interview with Ken and Ella Townsend: Stories of the land, the towers, the fire wardens and Native American houses." Conducted in July 2000 by Katherine Kane, Kent, New York.

Kipling, Rudyard. "The Gipsy Trail," *The Century*, vol. 45, issue 2 (Dec 1892).

MacCracken, Henry Noble. Old Dutchess Forever! The Story of An American County. New York: Hastings House, 1956.

Mann, Charles C. 1491: New Revelations of the Americas Before Columbus. New York: Vintage Books, 2005.

Merritt, Ralph. Oral History of Mt. Nimham, Kent, New York, 2009.

Murray, Jean and Osborn, Penny Ann. "Indians Who Lived Here Centuries Ago." An Historic Biographical Profile of the Town of Kent, Putnam County, New York, Town of Kent Bicentennial Committee, 1976.

New York State Census, 1845

New York State Census, 1915

New York State Census, 1925

O'Connor, R.F. "1854 Map of Putnam County." Putnam County Historian's Office.

Parker, Arthur C. "The Archaeological History of New York, Part Two." New York State Museum Bulletin, Nos. 237,238, Albany, New York, 1922.

PlanPutnam.org

Pritchard, Evan T. Native New Yorkers: The Legacy of the Algonquin People of New York. San Francisco, CA: Council Oak Books, LLC, 2002.

Pritchard, Evan T. "People of Manitou." Internet: http://peopleofmani tou.blogspot.com/, 2000-2006.

Pritchard, Evan T. No Word for Time: The Way of the Algonquin People. San Francisco, CA: Council Oak Books, LLC, 2001.

Putnam County Courier, 1841-2009: Reed Memorial Library, Carmel New York.

Reed, Thomas H. "1876 Map of Kent." Putnam County Historian's Office.

Rickert-Shatz Family, Oral History Regarding Stephen Wood Cornell and the Fairview Farm on Mt. Nimham, 2004-2009.

Ritchie, William A. An Introduction to Hudson Valley Prehistory. Albany: State Museum and Science Service Bulletin #367, 1958. Reprinted 1969.

Roberts, James A. New York in the Revolution as Colony and State. Albany NY: Weed-Parsons Printing Company, 1897.

Ruttenber, E.M. The Indians of Hudson's River. Albany NY: J. Munsell & Co., 1872.

Shorto, Russell. The Island at the Center of the World. New York: Doubleday Publishing, Inc., 2004.

Smalley Family Genealogy, Laura Brody (descendant of Isaiah Smalley), 2005.

Smalley Family Genealogy, Putnam County Historian's Office, 2004.

Smith, J. Michael. "The Highland King Nimhammaw and the Native Indian Proprietors of Land in Dutchess County, NY: 1712-1765." The Hudson River Valley Review, Vol. XVII, No. 2, September 2000, pp. 69-108.

Smith, Philips H. General History of Dutchess County from 1609 to 1876. New York, New York, 1876.

Sultzman, Lee. Wappinger History. Internet: http://www.dickshovel .com/wap.html, 1997.

Tarbox, Gilbert Cryinghawk. Daniel Nimham and the Wappinger People of the Hudson Valley. Kent NY: Gilbert Cryinghawk Tarbox, 2004.
Town of Kent Bicentennial Committee. An Historic Biographical Profile of the Town of Kent, Bicentennial Edition. Kent NY: Kent Historical Society, 1976.

Town Records of Frederickstown/Kent, 1788-1841, Putnam County Historian's Office, 2004.

Townsend, Ella. Reveries: Vignettes of Seven Decades in Putnam County. Beacon NY: Watkins Press, 1989.

Townsend, Stephen Kenneth. Oral History Regarding Mt. Nimham, Kent, NY, 1998-2000.

U.S. Census, 1790

U.S. Census, 1800

U.S. Census, 1810

U.S. Census, 1820

U.S. Census, 1830

U.S. Census, 1840

U.S. Census, 1850

U.S. Census, 1860

U.S. Census, 1870

U.S. Census, 1880

U.S. Census, 1890

U.S. Census, 1900

U.S. Census, 1910

U.S. Census, 1920

U.S. Census, 1930

U.S. Geological Survey Map of 1894, U.S. Dept. of the Interior

U.S. Geological Survey Map of 1928, U.S. Dept. of the Interior

U.S. Geological Survey Map of 1944, U.S. Dept. of the Interior

USDA Forest Service. Background Paper History: Historical Overview of the Southern Forest Landscape and Associated Resources. Wayne D. Carroll, Peter R. Kapeluck, Richard A. Harper, David H. Van Lear, Forest Resources Department, Clemson University, Internet: http://www.srs.fs.usda.gov/ sustain /draft/histry/histry-09.htm, 2004.

Vaughan, Alden T. Transatlantic Encounters: American Indians in Britain, 1500-1776. New York: Cambridge University Press, 2006.

Walling, Richard S. "Nimham's Indian Company of 1778." Internet: American Revolution.Org, http://www. americanrevolution.org/ ind2.html, 2008.

Walling, Richard S. "Death in the Bronx: The Stockbridge Indian Massacre, August 31, 1778." Journal of the Native American Institute, Columbia-Greene Community College; Vol. 1, No. 2, Spring 1998.

Wessels, Tom, Cohen, Brian D. and Zwinger, Ann. Reading the Forested Landscape: A Natural History of New England. New York: W.W. Norton & Company, Inc., 1997.

Wheeler, Glendon E. Index of Gravestones for the People of Putnam County. Simi Valley, California: Wheeler Historical Society; Rhinebeck, N.Y., 1997.

Whipple, George C. III, and White, Reginald. Town of Kent, New York: An Illustrated History. Wasco New Jersey: Whip-poor-Whit Enterprises, 2008.

Index

About the Author

Tom Maxson was born and raised on Long Island, New York, living for most of his youth in the beautiful and historic town of Huntington, made famous by the British capture of the patriot spy, Nathan Hale. As an early student of history, he was concerned by the negligent paving-over of its history, with little regard given for preservation or any long-term planning. After earning his business graduate degree from Adelphi University, in 1988 Tom moved with his family to Kent, New York, attracted by its great natural beauty and historic heritage. He joined the Kent Historical Society, and became very active in the Kent Conservation Advisory Committee, working on numerous preservation initiatives, including the documentation of the Brown-Barrett-Mead Farm, the reclamation of the old town roads, and the survey and documentation of the stone chambers in Kent. After retiring from

the corporate planning, marketing and financial analysis positions he held for nearly 30 years, in late 2007 he established *Highlands Preservation, Inc.*, a non-profit volunteer organization dedicated to the protection of historic and prehistoric sites in the Hudson Valley region. *Highlands Preservation* also works with local government and community groups to promote heritage tourism in order to stimulate their local economies, and to protect their property values. Tom was later selected to serve on his town's Master Plan Committee, assisting the Town Board in helping to establish the Town of Kent as the regional leader in historic preservation, promotion of its natural and heritage resources, and revitalization planning for its main economic corridor. In 2009, he was acknowledged with an award from the Putnam County Historian's Office for his preservation activities, and has been a featured speaker at historic preservation conferences and sym-posiums. For further information, please visit Highlands Preservation's website at: http://www.highlandspreservation.org/

His next book, *Whang Hollow: Sacred Valley of the Nochpeem*, is slated for publication in late 2010.

www.ingramcontent.com/pod-product-compliance
Lightning Source LLC
Chambersburg PA
CBHW021233090426
42740CB00006B/511

9 780578 025810